Tragic Glory

A Concise, Illustrated History
of the Civil War

By Douglas Lee Gibboney

Sergeant Kirkland's
Fredericksburg, Virginia

Copyright 1997 by Douglas Lee Gibboney

Published & Distributed by

Sergeant Kirkland's Museum
and Historical Society, Inc.

912 Lafayette Blvd., Fredericksburg, Virginia 22401-5617
Tel. (540) 899-5565; Fax: (540) 899-7643
E-mail: Civil-War@msn.com

Manufactured in the USA

The paper in this book meets the guidelines for permanence and
durability of the Committee on Production Guidelines for Book
Longevity of the Council on Library Resources, Inc.

Library of Congress Cataloging-in-Publication Data

Gibboney, Douglas Lee, 1953-
Tragic Glory: A Concise Illustrated History of the Civil War / by
Douglas Lee Gibboney. – 1st ed.
p.   cm.
Includes bibliographical references and index.
ISBN 1-887901-17-5 (alk. paper)
1. United States – History – Civil War, 1861-1865 – Pictorial works.
I. Title.
E468.7.G53   1997
973.7 – dc21   97-40362
                                                            CIP
First Edition
1 2 3 4 5 6 7 8 9 10

Cover design and page layout Ronald R. Seagrave
Edited by Pia S. Seagrave, Ph.D.

Cover illustration: Rothermel's *Charge of the Pennsylvania Reserves at Plum
Run*, courtesy of The State Museum of Pennsylvania, Pennsylvania Historical
and Museum Commission.

As always, to Carolyn.

An 1885 composite cabinet-card, entitled "The Confederate Commanders" widely circulated in the South to help Northern insurance companies to sell their policies. (Sergeant Kirkland's Museum and Historical Society)

Table of Contents

1864 Page 102

Turned Out of Our House/Kilpatrick's Richmond Raid/Grant Goes into the Wilderness/Spotsylvania: The Bloody Angle/Cold Harbor: The Battle Grant Would Always Regret/Sherman Captures Atlanta/I Am Willing to Come Home/CSS Alabama: Rebel Raider or Pirate Ship/Black Soldiers and the Fight for Freedom/The Burning of Chambersburg/Early and Sheridan in the Shenandoah/The Old Sixth Took Them in Hand/Custer: The Boy General/Trench War/Sherman's March to the Sea/Slaughter at Franklin; Disaster at Nashville

1865 Page 141

Sherman Moves North/Richmond Falls and Lee Surrenders/Lee's Farewell/ Assassination of Lincoln

Introduction

This book was written with the intention of offering an entertaining outline of the Civil War and, at the same time, of highlighting some of its most interesting incidents and personalities. It is intended to be enjoyable and informative whether the entire text is read straight through or whether the individual sections are taken at random.

Many introductory histories of the War Between the States justifiably run several hundred pages. This book purposely limits its length in order to provide a concise overview. As a result, many events, persons and details do not receive the attention they would deserve in a longer study. This is in no manner meant to diminish their importance; it is simply the dread matter of editing to form.

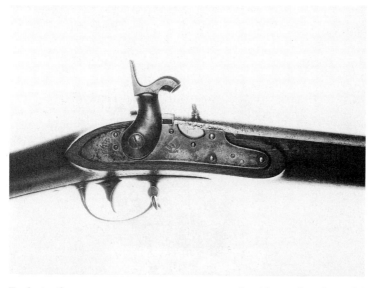

Early in the war, many troops were armed with outdated Model 1816 muskets, which had been converted from flintlock to percussion. The hammer would strike a brass cap placed on the nipple, sending a spark into the barrel to ignite the gunpowder. (Author's Collection. Photo by Brenda Goodhart.)

Many of the Union officers were as young and inexperienced as the men they commanded. (Author's Collection)

Acknowledgements

While the actual writing of a book may be a solitary pursuit, the task of bringing it to completion is very much a team effort. Everett K. Cooper, of New Cumberland, Pennsylvania, author of a number of articles on Civil War topics and one of my mentors when I first began studying the subject many years ago, graciously agreed to review the text before publication. Professor Michael Barton, of Pennsylvania State University at Harrisburg and author of *Goodmen: The Character of Civil War Soldiers*, kindly offered his comments as well. Mac Wyckoff of Spotsylvania, Virginia, who penned *A History of the 2nd South Carolina Infantry, 1861-1865*, and *A History of the 3rd South Carolina Infantry, 1861-1865* among others books and articles, also provided many insightful suggestions.

Brenda Goodhart of Dillsburg, Pennsylvania, shot several of the artifact photographs in the book. The staff of the U.S. Army Military Institute at Carlisle, Pennsylvania, assisted me in finding some of the less-common photos from their collection. Kevin Hardie, of Indianapolis, Indiana, and Alan Bailets, of Lemoyne, Pennsylvania, helped resolve my computer problems. The maps were created by Your Private Printer, Harrisburg, Pennsylvania.

Finally, my warmest thanks go to Dr. Pia S. Seagrave and Ronald R. Seagrave of Spotsylvania, Virginia. Dr. Seagrave patiently edited the entire text and helped repair my often inconsistent writing. As publisher, Mr. Seagrave has been in on this project from the beginning, devoting much time from his crowded schedule to making this volume a success.

Ever since I was a small child, I have been afflicted with Civil War disease. Even so, I am unable to satisfactorily explain the fascination it holds for me and for so many others. Nonetheless, I hope this volume will serve as a good introduction for those just getting the virus.

DLG

Virginia's statehouse, designed by Thomas Jefferson, hosted the Confederate Congress after Richmond became the Southern capital. (U.S. Army Military History Institute)

Prelude

How the Civil War Began...

The Divisive Issue of Slavery

There is no single simple answer to what caused the Civil War, but the dispute over slavery was a major contributing factor. By 1860, slavery was at the center of all social, economic and political debates. On the other hand, three-quarters of Southern families and perhaps ninety percent of all Southerners owned no slaves, so obviously the roots of this sectional conflict went beyond that lone issue.

The ownership of one human being by another human being had been a part of civilization since ancient times. In 1619, Dutch traders brought the first captive Africans to Virginia. When the United States was founded on the principles of life, liberty and the pursuit of happiness, the system of human bondage was already a long-established practice. In 1774, however, Rhode Island abolished slavery, becoming the first American colony to do so.

Slavery was a sticking point in the writing of the Constitution. Arguing over representation in Congress, the founding fathers decreed that slaves would represent three-fifths of a person, a compromise designed to keep harmony between the rapidly industrializing North and the agriculture-dependent South.

In 1807, Congress prohibited the importation of new slaves from Africa. This, however, did not prevent existing slaves from being bred to increase the number of persons in bondage. Human chattel had become essential to the prosperity of the antebellum plantation economy.

Through the first half of the 19th century, tensions grew in Congress and between the North and South over this issue. New states were admitted to the Union so as to keep an even balance between freeman and slave. The Missouri Compromise of 1820 gave statehood to both Maine and Missouri, even though the latter state lay beyond the traditional line boundaries separating North and South. In the future, however, slavery was to be banned north of Missouri's southern border.

This artificial line would have dire implications for the future as American settlers moved west. From his retirement at Monticello, Thomas Jefferson called the compromise a "firebell in the night," correctly foreseeing the conflict it could cause.

Robert Edward Lee (Library of Congress)

By 1846, all Northern states had outlawed slavery though racial intolerance remained; for example, Abraham Lincoln's home state of Illinois prohibited freed blacks from residing within its borders. That same year, the Supreme Court ruled that Dred Scott, an escaped slave recaptured in a free state, must be returned South to captivity.

When Congress passed the Compromise of 1850, California entered the Union as a free state while the South received a stricter fugitive slave law and promises that the Southwest territories would not ban slavery. This compromise papered over the cracks which were dividing the country and held the Union together for another decade.

During the 1850s, violence flared in Kansas as the artificial boundaries of the Missouri Compromise were challenged. Slaveholders fought free staters in an undeclared war to determine what the status of Kansas would be.

Abolitionist John Brown had been active in the Kansas fighting. But, coming back east, he shocked the nation in October 1859 with a raid on Harpers Ferry, Virginia--now West Virginia. In a move both poorly conceived and poorly executed, the zealot Brown led a rag-tag band of followers to capture the United States Arsenal at the confluence of the Potomac and Shenandoah Rivers. He hoped that arming and freeing slaves in that area would set off a chain-reaction of insurrections across the South. A contingent of U.S. Marines under the command of Colonel Robert E. Lee soon stormed the fire house where Brown and his men had taken refuge. The South, which lived in fear of a slave revolt, did not take Brown's transgression lightly. After a quick trial for treason against the Commonwealth of Virginia, Brown and several others were hung.

The Harpers Ferry Raid served notice that the conflict which Thomas Jefferson feared was on its way. Less than two years later, Union soldiers would march to war singing *John Brown's Body*.

States Rights Gist was born on September 3, 1831, in Union District, South Carolina, the son of a wealthy planter and future governor of the Palmetto State. In 1864, Gist was killed at the battle of Franklin, Tennessee. His horse had been shot out from under him, while he continued on foot towards the Federals. (U.S. Army Military History Institute)

The Question of States Rights

Slavery was far from the sole cause of the conflict. In creating a new nation, the founding fathers left unanswered many questions about the autonomy of the individual states, and these questions grew in importance as the economic differences between North and South increased.

For the industrial North, tariffs on foreign products lessened competition for its own manufactured goods. For Southern agriculture, these same tariffs increased the cost of merchandise it desired to import. South Carolina attempted to exempt itself from these national taxes, resulting in the Nullification Crisis of 1832. President Andrew Jackson, a Southerner, vowed to use force to uphold the federal law, but a compromise was found and the crisis passed.

Interestingly, prior to the Civil War, people often referred to the country in the plural; for example, the United States are instead of the United States is. Many believed that, just as a state had freely entered the union, it also had the right to freely leave. New England Federalists, for example, seriously considered secession after the election of Thomas Jefferson to the presidency in 1800 and continued to do so through the War of 1812.

Fiery rhetoric from leaders on both sides pushed the country toward dissolution. By 1860, the national discord produced a four-way race for the presidency. In results mirroring the regional disagreements, the four-year-old Republican party captured the White House for the first time with forty percent of the popular vote. The Republican candidate, Abraham Lincoln, was viewed in the South as an extreme abolitionist and, in the months prior to Lincoln's inauguration, South Carolina led a string of Southern states out of the Union.

Yet, as the nation moved toward war with itself, we would do well to consider why the average soldier rushed to arms. As has been noted, most Southerners did not own slaves; they enlisted to protect their homes from invasion by the Yankees. Similarly, many Northerners rallied to the colors not to end slavery but to preserve the Union.

For whatever reason, they fought; the resulting conflict was long and bloody.

Jefferson Finis Davis, the first and only chief executive of the Confederate States of America. (U.S. Army Military History Institute)

Two Sons of Kentucky

Jefferson Davis and Abraham Lincoln were both born in the Commonwealth of Kentucky in 1808 and 1809, respectively. Though their arrival in the world was separated by less than a year and one hundred miles, they grew up under very different circumstances. Davis' family moved to Mississippi where he became a planter, politician and Mexican War hero. Lincoln's family headed north to Indiana and Illinois in an attempt to escape a hard-scrabble existence.

Lincoln raised himself from obscurity almost through sheer force of will. Largely self-educated, he became a lawyer, served in the Illinois legislature, and won a single term in the U.S. House of Representatives, the only federal political office he had held before his election as sixteenth president of the United States.

Davis graduated from West Point and served alongside Lincoln in the U.S. House of Representatives. Resigning to lead Mississippi volunteers in the War with Mexico, he suffered a severe wound at the Battle of Buena Vista. Afterward, Davis won election to the U.S. Senate and was appointed Secretary of War under Franklin Pierce. As war clouds gathered, he once again represented Mississippi in the Senate.

When Southern delegates met in Montgomery, Alabama, to form the Confederate nation, Davis emerged as the new country's first--and ultimately only--president. The top job was not Davis' preferred choice; instead, he had hoped for an army field command.

Abraham Lincoln, 16th President of the United States. (Author's Collection)

Possibly one of the earliest wartime photographs of Pierre Gustave Toutant Beauregard, this shows him in uniform as a colonel of engineers in the Provisional Army of Louisiana, and was taken about February 1861. (U.S. Army Military History Institute)

1861

Fort Sumter: The First Shots of War

As the Confederacy took shape, much of the U.S. property within her borders quickly fell to the Rebel forces. A handful of forts, however, were not easily taken; and among these was Fort Sumter, guarding Charleston Harbor in South Carolina. Major Robert Anderson, with his garrison of 127 men, had been in a virtual state of siege since December 1860. Sitting on their tiny island, Sumter's defenders could only watch as a supply ship, *The Star of the West*, was fired upon in January. After that, negotiations between the Confederates and Washington produced a stalemate.

Major Anderson's dwindling supply of food meant that he would have to abandon the fort by April 15. But the crisis built to its own conclusion and, at 4:30 a.m. on April 12, 1861, Confederate General Pierre Gustave Toutant Beauregard ordered his cannons to open fire on Sumter. Ironically, Beauregard had been Major Anderson's star artillery pupil at West Point.

Who among the Rebels fired the first shot of the war remains a matter of argument, though 67-year-old Edmund Ruffin remains a traditional contender for the honor. Ruffin, a renowned Virginia agriculturist and writer, was such an ardent Southern nationalist that he fired a bullet into his own brain when Confederate fortunes failed four years later.

This opening battle at Fort Sumter was exciting, colorful and nearly bloodless. While the members of Charleston society watched from their rooftops, Anderson's men resisted the Confederate bombardment until the evening of the thirteenth. On the following morning, the defenders fired a ceremonial hundred-gun salute as they lowered their flag and prepared to hand over the fort. During the ceremony, the war took its first casualty when an artillery explosion accidentally killed Private Daniel Hough.

Abraham Lincoln, on April 15, called for 75,000 troops to provide ninety-days service in suppressing the rebellion. This action incited four more Southern states to pass ordinances of secession and to join the seven states that had already left the Union.

The eleven Confederate States were South Carolina, Mississippi, Florida, Alabama, Georgia, Louisiana, Texas, Virginia, Arkansas, Tennessee and North Carolina. Two other states, Kentucky and Missouri, organized secessionist governments and were represented in the thirteen stars on the Confederate flag.

After the firing upon Fort Sumter, the Confederacy tried to establish a national anthem. This illustrated song sheet cover of George H. Miles' *God Save the South* appeared on one of several editions of the song. (Library of Congress)

PENNSYLVANIA

✪ Harrisburg

N.J.

GETTYSBURG ✕

ANTIETAM

● Baltimore

HARPERS FERRY
WINCHESTER
CEDAR CREEK
BALL'S BLUFF
CHANCELLORSVILLE

MONOCACY

✪ Washington, D.C.

MANASSAS

DEL.

W. VA.

MD.

THE WILDERNESS ✕
VIRGINIA

FREDERICKSBURG
SPOTSYLVANIA COURT HOUSE

Richmond ✪

SEVEN PINES/SEVEN
DAYS/COLD HARBOR

SAYLERS CREEK
APPOMATTOX ✕
COURT HOUSE

PETERSBURG

FIVE FORKS

✪ Raleigh

✕ BENTONVILLE

NORTH CAROLINA

Wilmington ●

✕ FORT FISHER

✪ Columbia
SOUTH
CAROLINA

ATLANTIC OCEAN

Charleston ●
✕ FORT SUMTER

Savannah ●
✕ FORT PULASKI

EASTERN THEATER
1861-1865

Murder at the Marshall House

In the spring of 1861, 24-year-old Colonel Elmer Ellsworth was a national celebrity. Before the war, he had turned the U.S. Zouave Cadets of Chicago into a crack championship drill team and took them on a tour of major cities in the Northeast. In colorful French-style uniforms that featured white gaiters, short jackets and baggy red pants, they won rave reviews for their swift and intricate military maneuvers.

Ellsworth returned to Illinois, studying law in the office of Abraham Lincoln and campaigning for him in the presidential election of 1860. When Lincoln went to Washington to assume office, Ellsworth accompanied him as a bodyguard.

With the advent of war, Ellsworth recruited the 11th New York Fire Zouaves, so named because many of their members were New York City firemen. To defend against an anticipated secessionist attack, the regiment rushed to Washington. They were quartered in the capitol rotunda and made general nuisances of themselves, climbing down ropes suspended from the dome and even using their bayonets to attack Jeff Davis' old desk in the Senate.

On May 24, the day after Virginia officially left the Union, Ellsworth's men sailed across the Potomac River to occupy Alexandria. The unit disembarked and marched a few blocks up King Street where the Confederate Stars and Bars were flying above the Marshall House Hotel. Ellsworth ran into the building with four of his men and cut down the flag.

As they descended the staircase, innkeeper James Jackson pointed a double-barreled shotgun at them. One of the soldiers batted at the weapon with his musket, but Jackson fired, killing Ellsworth. Seconds later, Jackson fell dead from a Union gunshot. His enraged Fire Zouaves threatened to burn the town and had to be confined that night on a ship in the middle of the Potomac.

In the North, Ellsworth became a martyr as the first Federal officer to die in the war. At Lincoln's instruction, an honor guard carried the body to lie in state at the White House.

Strong, well-manned Federal fortifications like this would inflict heavy casualties upon any attacking force.
(U.S. Army Military History Institute)

"I Herd the Mornefool Sound of the Drums When You Left..."

As the men went off to war, the women, the children and the blacks, were left behind. Though the writing style is clearly of another era, this letter by Lysaneas L. Conrad of Salem, North Carolina, expresses the timeless emotions felt when a loved one marches to battle.

Forsyth Co., N.C.
July the 6th 1861

Dear Sandy

I take my pen in hand to drop you a few lines to inform you that I am well hoping they will find you in the same sate of health. I received your letter on the 5th it afforded me a great deal of pleasure for it was the first I herd from you since you left Salem. I herd the mornefool sound of the drums when you left Salem it made me feel very sorry to hear you leave perhaps to return no more. I have lonesome times but it is no more than can be expected being deprived from the only one that I love. You sed that you wanted me to say that I had not forgotten you. You many be well assured that I have not for of days. You occupy my thoughts and of nights you are the object of my dreams.

When this you see remember me though many miles apart my pen is bad my ink is pale my love to you shall never fail. When from home receding and from hearts that ache to bleeding. Think of those you left who love thee think how long the night will be. to the eyes that weep for thee. God bless and keep thee I have no more to say at present. I must bring my few lines to a close

I remain your affectionate friend

Lysaneas L. Conrad

Irvin McDowell was the commander of the Union forces at First Bull Run. (U.S. Army Military History Institute)

The First Fighting at Bull Run

The best days of war are always at the beginning, before anyone realizes what an awful and serious business has been undertaken.

So it was in the spring and early summer of 1861 as civilians-turned-soldiers rushed to army camps around Washington and the newly anointed Confederate capitol at Richmond, Virginia.

In the North, newspaper headlines urged the recruits on to Richmond while the Southern army contemplated benign defensive operations which reflected Jeff Davis' policy that "...all we want is to be let alone."

By mid-July, the public and political pressure for action by the Union army could no longer be resisted. What's more, many of the soldiers' ninety-day enlistments would soon expire without them ever having seen action.

Accordingly, Brigadier General Irvin McDowell led his inexperienced and poorly prepared troops toward Manassas Junction, some twenty miles from Washington, where the equally ill-trained Rebels waited.

On Sunday, July 21, the two amateur armies fought a fierce see-saw battle along the waters of Bull Run. The fighting could have gone either way, but it ended in a Union rout. For the first time in the history of warfare, a railroad had been used to achieve strategic mobility--bringing troops from the Shenandoah Valley just in time to contribute to the Confederate success.

The Union army fled back to the defenses of Washington, taking in its wake a large group of civilian sightseers who had packed picnic lunches and journeyed out for an enjoyable afternoon of watching men kill one another. Pursuing Confederates captured and imprisoned one such frolicker, U.S. Congressman Alfred Ely of New York.

The hero of Fort Sumter, Pierre G.T. Beauregard, shared victory honors with General Joe Johnston, but another Confederate officer also gained his first taste of fame. In the early part of the battle, events went badly for the South, but the brigade of Thomas Jonathan Jackson held its ground. Seeing this, Brigadier General Barnard Bee shouted to his men, "Look! There stands Jackson like a stonewall. Rally behind the Virginians!"

Bee did not survive the fighting of that hot summer day, but his words gave "Stonewall" Jackson a nickname that became immortal.

Southern Dreams, Northern Might

The success at Bull Run spawned a wave of optimism in the Confederacy that the war would be short and independence easily achieved. A Rebel victory at Wilson's Creek, Missouri, on August 10, bolstered this feeling and raised hopes that that state could soon be firmly locked into the new Southern nation.

In the North, however, the mood was much different. There was a realization that restoring the Union might require substantial treasure, toil, and blood.

The Rebel leaders believed that European dependence on American cotton provided the leverage for bringing much-needed foreign recognition to their new nation. "King Cotton" amounted to more than half of all U.S. exports before the war; seven-eighths of the world's cotton supply grew in Dixie.

But the Confederate government failed to foresee that growers in other nations, such as in Brazil, would seize this opportunity to gain market share, and that Lincoln's naval blockade of Rebel ports would eventually strangle the South's ability to export its cash crop. The Confederates also underestimated the repugnance many Europeans felt toward slavery.

Indeed, an independent observer comparing the resources of North and South would find little reason for Confederate confidence.

The North contained a population of twenty-two million people; the South had just over nine million and more than a third of those were slaves. A steady flow of European immigration also added to Northern manpower. Eventually, the Union fielded over two million soldiers while the Southern armies had somewhere between 600,000 and 900,000 men.

In the North, there were 110,000 manufacturing facilities; the South had only 18,000. Ninety-seven percent of all American firearms came from the North as did the majority of all railroad equipment. In 1861, the North had a railroad network of 22,385 miles; the South had only 8,783 miles, which it struggled to keep in repair during the war.

For firearms, the South relied upon prewar inventory, foreign imports and battlefield captures. Much of the Confederacy's limited domestic firearms production came from manufacturing equipment removed from the United States Arsenal at Harpers Ferry.

Nevertheless, the Confederacy initially planned to fight a purely defensive war, and its armed forces included many of the best officers from the prewar army. In that summer of 1861, anything seemed possible.

"I Like It Very Well So Far..."

Pennsylvanian Abraham Wolf was one of thousands of Northerners who rushed to enlist following the defeat at Bull Run. This is his first letter home.

Camp Curtin
August 22nd 1861

Dear father

    I now take my pencil to inform you a few lines about how I am getting along in the camp. I am getting along well. We arrived here yesterday at 4 o'clock and then we look for a place to sleep all night. Then we found a board shanty and there we stopped and got our dinners. We had bread and baloney sausage and it was very good and then we walked around in camp till night and then we got our blankets and went to bed. We have boards fixed 2½ feet from the ground and these we laid on and slept very comfortable and father I let you know I never had as much pleasure a riding on the cars from Sunbury to Harrisburg and further I let you know their ain't many soldiers in camp just now but they are coming in very fast again. And further I let you know that we were sworn in the camp today and we were also examined and we were all sound except three and they were rejected. And further I let you know what we have to eat the best kind of bread and beef and beans and rice and coffee. I have also drunk more coffee since I am down here than I did in five years because they made me drink it on account of the change of water. And further I let you know that we will be uniformed and also armed till Saturday the 24th of August. And further I let you know what kind of kitchen we have. We also have a tin-cups, pewter plates, knives and forks and table spoons and so on.

    And further I let you know I like it very well so far and we don't know yet when we will leave this camp. And also I whope these few may find you as well as myself and so I must come to a close for this time and I don't see it necessary for you to write. I may not get the letter because we have nothing arranged yet so goodbye.

Very truly yours Abr. Wolf
Henry W. Wolf

All Quiet Along the Potomac

In the East, after Bull Run, little military action of consequence occurred for the balance of the year except for a minor October battle at Ball's Bluff, Virginia, where the Rebels chased a Yankee expedition into the Potomac River. Senator-turned-soldier Edward Baker, a friend of President Lincoln, died in that fighting. His corpse received the honor of a White House funeral.

On the strength of some small victories gained in western Virginia, Lincoln brought in Major General George Brinton McClellan to command the Union Army of the Potomac. Hailed as the "Young Napoleon," the West Pointer spent months forging his raw recruits into a real fighting force. In the process, he won their undying devotion. McClellan fully proved his organizational talents that fall and winter, but popular acclaim enlarged a troublesome ego, which would contribute mightily to his future downfall.

Viewing himself as the country's savior, McClellan felt free to both argue with and ignore his commander-in-chief. In fact, one night Lincoln called at McClellan's residence only to be told that the general was out. The president said he would wait. Later, a servant brought word that the general had returned but was retired for the evening. Lincoln endured such insults--at least for a time.

Across the Potomac, Confederates under Joe Johnston occupied hills which gave them a view of the partially completed U.S. Capitol dome and the unfinished Washington Monument. Disorganized by victory after Bull Run, the grey army failed to follow its advantage and now could only wait outside the Washington defenses, which grew stronger every day.

In camp, soldiers of both armies learned firsthand that more of them would die from illness than in battle. Smallpox, measles, dysentery and other diseases all took their toll.

The soldiers themselves were young, mainly between 18 and 30 years of age. Southerners in general were better acquainted with shooting and riding than their Northern counterparts; however, the era's Napoleonic tactics relied more upon blocks of firepower than individual marksmanship, and, by the war's end, the prowess of bluecoated horsemen would exceed that of the worn-down grey cavalry.

For the infantry, the standard weapon was a single-shot, muzzle loading musket which fired a .58 or .69 caliber bullet. Many on both sides carried prewar guns with smoothbore barrels though, as the conflict progressed, most obtained rifled muskets which offered superior long-range accuracy. That accuracy increased killing power so much that, by mid-war, the troops discarded their initial disdain of earthworks and dug in at the earliest opportunity.

To load and fire a musket, the soldier would first tear off the end of a paper cartridge, which was why recruits were required to have good teeth. He would then pour the gunpowder down the barrel and use a ramrod to push a lead bullet, called a Minié ball, on top of the powder. When the trigger was pulled, the hammer of the gun would strike a brass cap which provided the spark to ignite the gunpowder. In the heat of battle, soldiers often forgot to remove ramrods before firing and thus sent long metal arrows whistling toward the enemy. In addition to his musket, an infantryman would carry a cartridge box, bayonet, blanket, haversack, canteen and, perhaps, a knapsack. Many soldiers entered the war with extra weapons, such as pistols and big bowie knives, but these were soon discarded as unnecessary during long marches.

The uniforms were wool, comfortable in winter but a poor choice for summer when most of the campaigning took place. In general, the Union armies obtained sufficient supplies for their enlisted men to wear the regulation dark blue sack coat and sky blue pants. A Yankee private received $13 a month, later increased to $16 a month.

Confederates did not fare as well. Regulations called for a cadet grey coat with sky blue trousers, but many Confederates wore whatever was available. Homespun butternut uniforms were common and, in the winter, captured Yankee overcoats became popular. A private received $11 a month until 1864, when inflation brought a raise to $18. Interestingly, it can be argued that much of the Confederate supply problem rose not from a lack of availability but from a lack of proper distribution.

Following Napoleon's famous maxim that an army marches on its stomach, the Union forces generally had the advantage in both quantity and quality of food. However, Confederates, usually fighting on their home ground, found it easier to approach friendly locals for a home-cooked meal. Both sides foraged liberally from neighboring farms, regardless of whether or not they had their commander's permission.

Army rations centered on staples such as beef, pork, and beans. Fresh bread would sometimes appear in camp but, on the march, rough square biscuits of "hardtack" were issued. Coffee and tobacco were seen as the essentials of existence. Confederate troops, having a home-grown abundance of the latter, frequently traded with the enemy for the former, which was kept out of the South by Lincoln's naval blockade.

Northern soldiers supplemented their diet with purchases from the wagons of sutlers who followed the army and who offered a wide variety of luxury goods at inflated prices. There were few sutlers in the South, though troops on the march were often met by vendors with kegs of cider or wheelbarrows full of meat-pies.

Running the Blockade

Shortly after the fall of Fort Sumter, Abraham Lincoln ordered the U.S. Navy to blockade all Southern ports in an effort to cut off supplies to the rebellious states. This would also prevent the Confederacy from raising cash by selling cotton to overseas markets.

At the beginning, the blockade was more concept than reality. There simply were not enough ships to cover 3500 miles of coastline. In the first year of the war, nine blockade runners arrived safely for every one the Federals captured. The North even tried unsuccessfully to seal off Rebel waterways by sinking its own obsolete ships in the sailing channels.

Uncle Sam's naval noose tightened as the war progressed. More and better blockading vessels were added until the total fleet reached six hundred. What's more, as Southern ports fell to Union arms, there were fewer and fewer harbors to blockade.

By 1864, only one out of every three blockade runners successfully slipped through the Union dragnet. Nevertheless, sea captains continued to try. After all, the profits which could be made were fabulous. Given its limited industrial base, the Confederacy would pay dearly for the imported armaments it needed to wage war. Even basic commodities, such as salt and coffee, brought many times the price for which they were purchased in the smuggler's stronghold of the Bahamas.

Blockade runners sat low in the water and were painted to blend in with the skyline. They burned anthracite coal so that no smoke would reveal their whereabouts to the enemy. Their crews, generally, were an international mix of seafarers with profit, not patriotism, as their primary motive. In the novel, *Gone With the Wind*, rakish Rhett Butler speculated in the blockade trade. The Southern navy, however, did use its own ships to import some heavier and less profitable munitions and materials that commercial blockade runners overlooked.

Confederate efforts to lift the blockade never really amounted to much. The Rebels lacked the ships to seriously challenge the North. However, the Confederates did develop a crude submarine, the *H.L. Hunley*, which managed to suffocate three crews before blowing up the *U.S.S. Housatonic* in Charleston Harbor in February 1864. The explosion also sank the *Hunley* and sent a fourth crew to a watery grave.

The game of running the blockade continued until the end of the war. In January 1865, Fort Fisher in North Carolina fell to a massive Union assault, and the Confederacy's last remaining eastern seaport at Wilmington closed to the outside world. Galveston, Texas, however, continued to receive blockade runners through May 1865.

Mrs. Rose O'Neal Greenhow (1814–1863), had a home opposite St. John's Church in view of the White House. The "beautiful rebel of Sixteenth Street," and her daughter were photographed in the courtyard of the Old Capitol Prison after protesting her "house arrest." (Library of Congress)

Rose Greenhow: Rebel Spy

Despite being the Federal capital, Washington, D.C. was very much a Southern city in 1861. Throughout the conflict, spy networks spirited much military information to Rebel leaders in Virginia.

One of the most celebrated undercover operatives of the early war was Rose O'Neal Greenhow. A native of Maryland and a fixture of Washington society, the Widow Greenhow had known nine U.S. presidents, but her heart lay with the Confederacy. Using social contacts and suitors to gain information, she sent General Beauregard advance word of the Union movement toward Bull Run. Detective Allen Pinkerton arrested Mrs. Greenhow the following month, and, after a stay in Old Capitol Prison, she was banished to the Confederacy in 1862.

The Confederate government hoped to use Greenhow's celebrated status for diplomatic advantage and dispatched her to Europe, where she met with France's Napoleon III and Britain's Queen Victoria. Returning to the Confederacy in September 1864, her ship ran aground near Wilmington, North Carolina, while being pursued by a Union vessel. Fearing a return to prison, Greenhow drowned in an attempt to reach shore, pulled underwater by the $2000 in gold coins in her skirt.

"Secesh" women leaving Washington for Richmond. (Library of Congress)

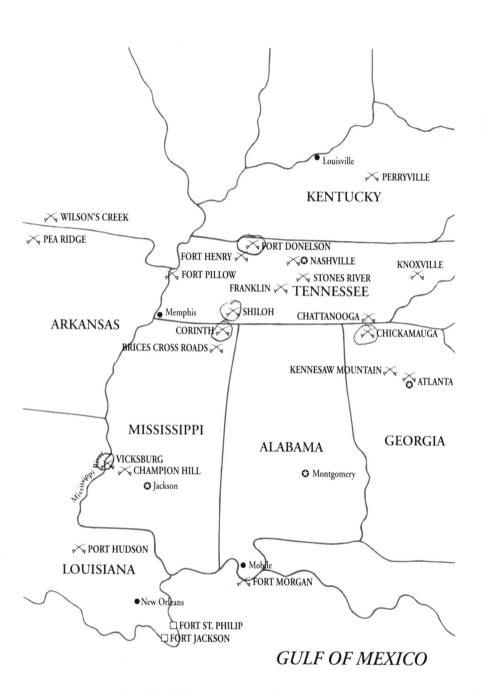

WESTERN THEATER
1861-1865

1862

Bloody Shiloh

In the early months of the new year, Confederate optimism waned as the North began flexing its might in Kentucky and Tennessee. Confederate General Albert Sidney Johnston commanded a poorly equipped and badly outnumbered Rebel army that was to defend a department stretching west from the Appalachian Mountains to the Indian Territories.

Johnston came with sterling credentials and a life-long background in military affairs. A graduate of West Point, he'd fought in the Black Hawk and Mexican Wars, served as a brevet brigadier general in the old army, and was a friend of Jefferson Davis. As the war drew near, Johnston commanded the Department of the Pacific in California. Learning that his adopted state of Texas had left the Union, Johnston resigned his commission and came across the continent to cast his lot with the Confederacy.

The man who was to prove Johnston's undoing held a lesser reputation. Ulysses Simpson Grant also had graduated from West Point and fought with distinction in the Mexican War, but then the isolation and boredom of frontier life at an army post exacerbated a weakness for alcohol. Eventually, Grant resigned from the military and tried, with little success, to make his way as a civilian. At one point, he peddled firewood on the streets of St. Louis. The advent of war found him clerking in his father's Galena, Illinois, dry goods store. Given the need for experienced officers, Grant became colonel of an infantry regiment and, two months later, jumped to brigadier general of volunteers.

In February 1862, Grant led the army wing of a joint operation with the navy against Confederate Fort Henry on the Tennessee River. Though it was one of the keys to the Southern defense line, Fort Henry instilled little confidence in its commander, Lloyd Tilghman, who sent most of his men to the stronger Fort Donelson, ten miles away on the Cumberland River. With only one hundred artillerymen, Tilghman remained behind to do battle.

On February 6, Yankee gunboats attacked the fort and destroyed thirteen of the fort's seventeen cannon. Tilghman surrendered even before Grant's foot soldiers could arrive.

Learning of the fort's fall, Albert Johnston elected to retreat south from Bowling Green, Kentucky, to Nashville, Tennessee. Though he believed that Fort Donelson was also doomed, Johnston, inexplicably, sent 12,000 men to reinforce the existing garrison of 5000.

On February 14, the Union navy sailed up the Cumberland River and made a failed assault against Rebel earthworks. The Union naval commander, Flag Officer Andrew Foote, suffered a wounded foot. Grant wondered whether he would be forced to lay siege to Donelson.

Despite victory over the enemy gunboats, little joy existed inside the Confederate fort for Grant's army was sealing off any route of retreat. The Confederates decided to fight their way out and launched an attack on the morning of the 15th. They succeeded in opening the road to Nashville, but the Confederate commanders, strangely, gave up their advantage and ordered their men back into the fort to regroup. That night, they decided to surrender.

After that decision was made, however, the top two Confederate generals, John Floyd and Gideon Pillow, abandoned their armies and escaped in a boat across the Cumberland River. Floyd had been the U.S. Secretary of War under James Buchanan and feared that he would be hung as a traitor if captured. Many Northerners believed he had purposely shipped weapons to Southern arsenals in anticipation of the hostilities.

So it fell to Simon Buckner, a prewar army chum of Grant's, to ask the bluecoats for terms. Grant quickly replied, "No terms but unconditional and immediate surrender can be accepted." Backed into a corner, Buckner agreed.

But not all Donelson's defenders were resigned to their fate. A former Memphis slave trader, Lieutenant Colonel Nathan Bedford Forrest, found a way out. He led his regiment of cavalry through icy waters in predawn darkness until they reached safety. Without any military training, Forrest instinctively seemed to understand warfare, and this was only the first of his many accomplishments.

The fall of Forts Henry and Donelson ruined any hope the Confederates had of holding Tennessee. In Nashville, Albert Sidney Johnston gave orders for the city to be abandoned and started his army toward Alabama. Shortly thereafter, a Federal force under Brigadier General Don Carlos Buell entered the Tennessee capital, which became a Union stronghold and supply depot for the remainder of the war.

In the North, Grant's victory made him famous and the story spread that his initials, U.S., stood for Unconditional Surrender. He received a promotion to major general and began moving his army toward its next goal, capturing the rail center of Corinth, Mississippi.

By late March, Grant's Yankees had traveled by boat down the Tennessee River to Pittsburg Landing, just north of the Mississippi stateline and within striking distance of Corinth. Following orders from his department commander, Major General Henry Halleck, Grant then waited to be reinforced by Buell's army, which was en route from Nashville.

Albert Sidney Johnston saw this as his opportunity. He had gathered more than 40,000 soldiers in Corinth with the intention of overpowering Grant before Buell arrived. Otherwise, the Confederates would be outnumbered by almost two to one.

Johnston hoped to surprise the enemy camp at dawn on April 4, but a poorly coordinated march delayed the attack for two days. During that time, bluecoat troops positioned near Shiloh Church had various encounters with the grey and butternut soldiers massing just outside their lines. But their division commander, Brigadier General William Tecumseh Sherman, discounted these as rumors coming from inexperienced and nervous troops. Sherman, a West Pointer who, like Grant, had experienced a difficult civilian career, was recently returned to duty after suffering some sort of nervous breakdown. He did not want to jeopardize his position by relying on inaccurate reports.

Grant, too, felt no impending danger and wrote as much to his superior, Halleck. Never again would the Confederates so successfully deceive these two Northern generals as they did before the fight at Pittsburg Landing.

The battle began almost by accident when Union patrols collided with the Confederate skirmish line in the early hours of Sunday, April 6. By afternoon, the Confederate offensive had driven the Federals back toward Pittsburg Landing and the Tennessee River. But a hornet's nest of fierce, day-long resistance by the embattled bluecoats bought time for the rest of the army to create a new defensive line near the river. Supported by two gunboats, Grant used this position to regroup his army and to prepare for an offensive on the next day.

The Southerners, on the other hand, had lost their momentum after a long and bloody day of fighting. In the mid-afternoon, Albert Sidney Johnston fell wounded while the general's physician, at Johnston's order, was off treating other soldiers. Without medical care, Johnston, unnecessarily, bled to death. Command of the Confederate forces went to the hero of Fort Sumter, Pierre Beauregard. That very morning, fearing their presence was already known, Beauregard had argued that the army should return to Corinth without attacking the enemy.

Through the night, most of Buell's army arrived to reinforce Grant. On April 7, the Federals launched a counterattack and slowly beat back the Confederates. After another full day of carnage, Beauregard ordered his men to retreat. Badly outnumbered, the Rebels evacuated Corinth without a fight on May 30.

Ulysses Simpson Grant, who guided the North to its ultimate victory. (U.S. Army Military History Institute)

The name "Shiloh" comes from the Bible and means "place of peace." The terrible casualties of the battle that raged around that little log church in Tennessee shocked both North and South.

More than 3400 soldiers were killed, over 16,000 were wounded, and almost 4000 were captured or missing. By contrast, at Bull Run, less than 900 men died; the wounded totaled 2700 and about 1300 were captured or missing. After Shiloh, Americans began to realize just how long and costly the war had become.

The First Battle of Ironclads

Union sailors lounging on wooden ships in Hampton Roads, Virginia, beheld a most unusual sight about midday on March 8, 1862. Steaming towards them came a large ironclad vessel flying the Rebel flag. Though scarcely recognizable in its present form, this was the former *U.S.S. Merrimack*, which had been sunk when the Federals had evacuated the Norfolk Naval Yard the previous year.

The Southerners raised and rebuilt the *U.S.S. Merrimack*, dramatically modifying the hull and covering it with four-inch iron plate. Re-christened the *C.S.S. Virginia*, the ship no longer had sails, but lumbered along on strained engines at a top speed of five knots per hour. The *Virginia* carried ten large cannons and came with a cast-iron prow for ramming the enemy.

When what was once the *U.S.S. Merrimack* (left)--now called the *C.S.S. Virginia*--squared off with the 54-gun frigate *U.S.S. Cumberland* in March 1862, the *Virginia* punched a hole as large as the head of a "hogshead" in the side of the *Cumberland*. (Library of Congress)

Commodore Franklin Buchanan, who, before the war, had helped start the U.S. Naval Academy at Annapolis, guided his metal monster toward its first target, the *U.S.S. Cumberland*. En route, the *Virginia* took a close-range broadside from the guns of another ship, the *U.S.S. Congress*, but the shots had little effect. The Confederates rammed and sank the *Cumberland* and then turned their attention to the Congress.

Attempting to escape, the *Congress* grounded itself in shoal water. The two ships battled back and forth, until the *Congress* finally struck her colors.

The *U.S.S. Minnesota* seemed to be the next victim, but it had the luck to run aground where the Rebel ship could not reach it. As darkness fell, the *Virginia* withdrew, its path lit by the flames of the burning *Congress*.

On the next day, the Confederates came back to continue their carnage. However, as they approached the enemy, they were greeted by an even stranger vessel than their own; the Yankees had brought in an ironclad, widely described as looking like a cheese box on a raft.

This was the *U.S.S. Monitor*, the invention of Swedish immigrant John Ericsson and built from a design that, initially, had been rejected by the navy. Its revolving turret, all that could be seen above water, carried two 11-inch Dahlgren smoothbore cannons.

For four hours, the ironclads fought to no conclusion, neither being able to seriously damage the other. Eventually, each withdrew; the *Monitor* continued to protect the suddenly outdated wooden warships while the *Virginia* blocked any Union naval advance up the James River to Richmond.

Both of these ships, which had revolutionized naval warfare around the world, suffered sad ends. When Norfolk fell, the crew of the *Virginia* scuttled her to prevent her capture by the Yankees. Some months later, the *Monitor* sank in a storm off Cape Hatteras, North Carolina.

In this "modern" American war, railroads played an important strategic role. (U.S. Army Military History Institute)

The Great Locomotive Chase

In a bid to isolate and capture Chattanooga, Tennessee, Brigadier General Ormsby Mitchell sent twenty-two volunteers, dressed as civilians, to disable the Western & Atlantic railroad north from Atlanta. Led by Union spy James J. Andrews, the raiders seized a train engine, the *General* in Big Shanty, Georgia, on April 12 and chugged toward Chattanooga, planning to burn bridges and wreck the rails en route.

At first, pursuit of the raiders was laughable. Captain W.A. Fuller, conductor in charge of the train, and Anthony Murphy, a roundhouse foreman, started out after the Yankees on foot. Soon they impressed a handcar and crew in the effort and, later, transferred to an engine they encountered on a siding.

Meanwhile, Andrews and his men found that tearing up iron rails was slow work without proper tools. They were startled to hear a train whistle, evidence that someone was chasing them. The raiders rapidly finished pulling a rail and steamed away.

When Fuller reached the broken track, he was forced to abandon his engine and, once again, go forward on foot. But then Andrews made a fatal mistake; he gave the right-of-way to a south-board train, the *Texas*, mistakenly believing this would block any further pursuit on the single rail line.

Instead, Fuller took command of the *Texas*, pushing all but one of her cars onto a siding and running the engine backwards to continue the chase. A squad of Confederate soldiers rode shotgun in the lone box car.

From then on nothing seemed to go right for the Andrews raiders. The Rebels gave them no time to remove any more rails and, when they loosened boxcars, the *Texas* simply pushed them aside. Strewing crossties over the track slowed the Southerners somewhat but not nearly enough.

Finally the Yankees tried burning their last boxcar inside a covered bridge; the rainy day prevented the flames from causing any real damage. Out of wood and water, Andrews and his men; abandoned the *General* just south of Chattanooga on the Tennessee state-line.

In a matter of days, the raiders were captured. The Confederates hung Andrews and seven of his men; eight escaped from prison and six were later exchanged.

All of the raiders, except Andrews, who was a civilian, eventually received the Congressional Medal of Honor.

The Enemy on the Edge of Richmond

For Jefferson Davis, April was the cruelest month. Albert Sidney Johnston, his long-time friend and greatest hope as a general, lay dead and the much-needed victory at Shiloh had slipped away. Most of Tennessee, for the moment at least, was lost.

Hope for a Confederate Missouri had withered as well, following a defeat in March at Pea Ridge, Arkansas.

Manpower was also a concern; the need for it forced Davis to sign a military conscription act, prompting a protest from Georgia Governor Joe Brown, who felt that conscription encroached upon states' rights. It has been said--and it is at least partially true--that the Confederacy died of states' rights.

Worse news arrived from New Orleans. On April 24, Union Flag Officer David Farragut successfully slipped his ships past the secessionist strongholds at the mouth of the Mississippi River and forced the surrender of the South's largest city. This came on the heels of earlier reports that the Federals had captured Fort Pulaski in Georgia, effectively shutting down the port of Savannah.

Richmond, too, was seriously threatened. General McClellan had moved his Army of the Potomac by water to the Virginia peninsula where it encountered 10,000 Confederates under the command of Major General Prince John Magruder. McClellan, with 105,000 soldiers, thought Magruder's feeble force equaled his own and, for an entire month, laid siege to Magruder at Yorktown. This bought time for Joe Johnston's army to come from northern Virginia and prepare a defense of the Confederate capital.

Throughout May, McClellan's Yankees inched closer and closer to Richmond, until, finally, they were so close they could hear its church bells chime. McClellan's position straddled the swampy Chickahominy River; Johnston decided to take advantage of the terrain by attacking two isolated Yankee corps on the south side of the stream. Johnston's subordinates became confused with his complex verbal orders and the advantage of surprise disappeared. Two days of serious fighting at Seven Pines ended inconsequentially--except that Johnston suffered a serious wound.

For the Confederacy, this may have been the luckiest shot ever fired by a Federal soldier, for it was this shot which gave Robert E. Lee command of the force which he renamed the Army of Northern Virginia.

Robert E. Lee came from true Southern patrician stock. His father, "Light Horse Harry" Lee had served as a general under George Washington, and Robert had been born in 1807 at Stratford Hall, the family estate on Virginia's northern neck. When his father's fortunes faltered, the family relocated to a townhouse in Alexandria, and Robert, eventually, went on to West Point. After graduation, he married Mary Custis, the great-granddaughter of Martha Washington.

Lee served with distinction in the Mexican War and on the frontier in Texas with the U.S. Cavalry. When John Brown raided Harpers Ferry, Lee led the U.S. Marine contingent who captured the fiery abolitionist.

With the outbreak of the war, Lee declined an offer to command the Union army. Although he did not believe in secession, he felt that duty required him to follow the course of his native state.

His first Confederate field command came in western Virginia. He did not distinguish himself and was sent to oversee the building of fortifications along the Carolina and Georgia coasts. When Johnston fell wounded, Lee was serving in Richmond as military adviser to President Davis.

Lee's instincts were aggressive and, upon assuming command of the army, he looked for a way not just to defend Richmond but to destroy the enemy. To accomplish this, he turned to "Stonewall" Jackson, who was then in the midst of a magnificent campaign against several Union armies in the Shenandoah Valley.

Jackson had spent much of the winter headquartered at Winchester in the lower valley and within striking distance of the Maryland border. In March, Jackson's small army of 4200 attacked--and got whipped by-- Brigadier General James Shield's force of 9000 at Kernstown.

Nevertheless, the Confederate's aggressiveness raised Union fears about the safety of Washington and prevented more men from being moved to McClellan.

Lee, while still military adviser to Davis, had upped the ante by sending reinforcements to Jackson and by urging him to continue his demonstrations. The result was the legendary Valley Campaign of 1862. Jackson's fast-marching foot cavalry won five victories in five weeks during May and June. This success sent Jackson to the front rank of Southern commanders.

If Lee had patrician roots, Jackson's were plebeian. Born in 1824 in what was then Virginia and is now West Virginia, Jackson's parents died while he was young. An uncle raised the future general. Through hard work and determination, he overcame a lack of early education to graduate from West Point. He served with distinction in the Mexican War and, later, resigned from the army to teach at the Virginia Military Institute.

Jackson was a devout Presbyterian and was known for his eccentric ways. He did not confide in the officers under him and one, Richard Ewell, said he never saw Jackson approach without expecting an order to attack the North Pole.

To smash McClellan's army, Lee decided to bring Jackson's troops from the valley. Four weeks after the Battle of Seven Pines, McClellan was still making careful preparations to lay siege to Richmond while fretting about a Rebel army that he believed outnumbered his own.

In fact, the reverse was true. McClellan had 100,00 men, 30,000 above the Chickahominy River and 70,000 below it. Lee had 72,000 troops, which would increase to 90,000 when Jackson arrived. Lee ordered 25,000 men to hold the Yankees south of the muddy Chickahominy. The remainder of his army would combine with Jackson to overwhelm the enemy on the north side.

The plan called for more coordination than the Confederates could muster. Jackson, exhausted from weeks of active campaigning, never arrived on June 26 as he was supposed to. The other Confederates waited anxiously until late afternoon and then attacked anyway, suffering high casualties from the guns of the well-positioned Federals near Mechanicsville.

That night, the Federals withdrew to Gaines Mill where Jackson's troops finally appeared in time to take part in another bloody battle on June 27. This was followed by successive days of more hard fighting at places like Savage Station and White Oak Swamp. In the last battle of the series, Lee continued his offensive July 1 with poorly coordinated assaults against a strongly defended Union position on Malvern Hill.

The casualties on both sides were appalling but were higher for the Confederates as they had been consistently on the attack. The streets of Richmond filled with the wounded who were returning from the front.

Despite its high price in blood, the fighting of the Seven Days achieved Lee's goal; McClellan was beaten back from the gates of the Confederate capital. Through the rest of July, the Army of the Potomac remained inactive in camp on Harrison's Landing along the James River. Then, regiment by regiment, the troops boarded ships and sailed home to the defenses of Washington, which they'd left but a few months before .

Three Times Around the Yankee Army

With his plumed hat and colorful uniform, James Ewell Brown Stuart cut the ideal figure of a romantic cavalier. West Point trained, he had served under Lee in the old army before casting his lot with the Confederacy. At First Bull Run, Stuart, still wearing his blue, prewar uniform, led his Virginia cavalry on a daring charge that scattered the New York Fire Zouaves.

Greater fame came in June, 1862, when Lee asked Stuart to scout the location of McClellan's right flank. Gathering 1200 horsemen, Stuart traveled a 100-mile circle around 100,000 Yankees with the loss of only one man. Stuart brought back the information Lee wanted, though some critics argue that the ride helped alert McClellan to his exposed flank. Nevertheless, news of Stuart's adventure elated the South.

Stuart repeated his circle game in October, 1862, on a raid to Chambersburg, Pennsylvania, where he destroyed Union supplies and equipment. Afterward, Lincoln groused that Stuart had gone around McClellan twice and the third time would mean that "Little Mac" was out.

During the Gettysburg Campaign in 1863, Stuart tried the same trick again, but with less sanguine results. Liberally interpreting Lee's somewhat vague instructions, Stuart took most of his cavalry on a long and slow journey between the Union army and Washington. Not until the second day of the Gettysburg fighting did Stuart rejoin Lee; the "eyes and ears" of Lee's army had gotten lost.

Stuart's actions ignited a controversy which continues to the present day; did his absence cause the Confederate defeat at this crucial battle?

John Pope was out-generaled by Lee and Jackson at Second Bull Run. (U.S. Army Military History Institute)

John Pope and Second Manassas

Even before the failure of the Peninsula Campaign, Lincoln was becoming increasingly disappointed with McClellan and his endless requests for reinforcements. In the hope of finding a more aggressive commander, he brought Major General John Pope from the western theater to head up the hastily-created Army of Virginia, largely a reorganization of the troops that had been held in the Shenandoah Valley and northern Virginia.

Earlier that spring, Pope had won favor with his capture of 3500 Confederates on Island No. 10 in the Mississippi River. Reaching Virginia, he told his new soldiers that he had come from the West, where "...we have always seen the backs of our enemies." He remarked that his headquarters would be in the saddle. This brought snickers that his headquarters were where his hindquarters should be.

Pope did not win friends among the civilian population either. He issued orders authorizing his army to subsist upon the countryside and he held the local residents responsible for guerrilla attacks on Union soldiers and property. It has been said that Pope was the only Northern commander whom Robert E. Lee actually despised.

With McClellan's soldiers inactive, Lee dispatched Stonewall Jackson to go after Pope. On August 9, at Cedar Mountain, near Culpeper, Virginia, Jackson encountered a portion of Pope's army, 9000 men under the command of Major General Nathaniel Banks. Leading a total force of 24,000, Jackson found himself in the unusual position of greatly outnumbering his adversary. But, using nearly all his troops, Banks took the offensive. He launched a massive flank attack, which almost crumpled the Confederate line. Only after a day of hard fighting could Jackson claim the field as his own.

Confident that McClellan was truly abandoning Harrison's Landing, Lee took the rest of his army north and joined Jackson in facing Pope along the Rappahannock River. Defying traditional military teaching, Lee split his army in the face of the enemy and sent Jackson on a long march around Pope's right. Covering fifty miles in two days, Jackson's foot cavalry pounced upon the Union supply depot at Manassas Junction. Hungry Rebels had all they could ever wish for to eat and drink that evening.

Pope retreated, hoping to defeat Jackson before the Confederate general could reunite with Lee. However, Jackson took his troops to a concealed, wooded position along an unfinished rail line near the old battlefield of First Manassas. Then he waited for Pope--and Lee--to arrive.

The Young Napoleon and 1864 Presidential Candidate, George B. McClellan (U.S. Army Military Institute)

Fighting began when Jackson revealed his presence by shelling passing Yankees at Groveton on the evening of August 28. The next day, Pope pushed a series of poorly planned, piecemeal assaults against the Confederates. Despite the arrival of reinforcements from McClellan's army, these attacks failed to crack the steady grey line. Pope believed Jackson wanted to escape and join Lee. In fact, the opposite was true. Jackson hoped to hold Pope in place, away from the awesome Washington defenses, so that the Federals could be destroyed upon Lee's arrival.

Pope renewed his assaults on August 30, and the fighting grew so fierce that Rebels lacking ammunition heaved rocks at the advancing bluecoats. But again, Jackson's line held and Lee was now ready to strike. In the late afternoon, Lee sent troops, under the command of Major General James Longstreet, in an all-out advance on the Union left.

The surprised blue soldiers broke. Jackson's men left the cover of the rail line to join Longstreet's assault. The Union army found itself being pushed back, until a rearguard action could be organized on Henry Hill, the scene of heavy fighting during the First Battle of Bull Run.

John Pope's army was whipped. It retreated back to the ring of forts around the nation's capital while its commander was relieved and sent to fight Indians in Minnesota. General McClellan once again returned to favor, much to the delight of the rank-and-file who had always retained a real love for "Little Mac."

In the space of three months, Robert E. Lee had accomplished much, driving the enemy away from Richmond until it was back on the defensive around Washington. If there was disappointment, it was that he had failed in his efforts to destroy either McClellan or Pope. Lee knew he could not successfully breach the fortifications of the national capital, yet he was determined to retain the initiative and continue on the offensive. In order to do so, he turned toward Maryland.

Soldiers and Civilians stampede from the defeat of Federal troops at the battle of Bull Run. (Library of Congress)

A Union cannon crew at Fort Lyon, Virginia, in 1862. (U.S. Army Military History Institute)

Antietam: Lee's First Invasion

On September 4, the Army of Northern Virginia began crossing the Potomac River on its first invasion of the North. To the Confederates, it was not so much an invasion as it was a chance to liberate a sister state from the yoke of Yankee aggression.

However, the Rebels were disappointed by their lukewarm reception. Many Marylanders looked in dismay at the dirty and ragged condition of Lee's legions. Few volunteers flocked to enlist; in fact, Maryland eventually gave twice as many soldiers to the Union cause as it did to the Confederacy. Maryland was, of course, subject to the Federal draft.

The grey army camped just east of Frederick, while Lee looked at maps of Pennsylvania for opportunity. The stakes were high. Winning a decisive battle in the North could bring European recognition and assistance to the Confederate nation and mean an end to the war.

But first Lee needed to protect his lines of communication and supply by moving them to the west. There they would be shielded by the Blue Ridge and South Mountain ranges, and would be less exposed to enemy raiders.

Lee split his army. Longstreet marched over the mountains toward Hagerstown, while Jackson went off to capture Harpers Ferry and remove the threat of the Federal garrison posted there.

McClellan gingerly followed in the wake of Lee's troops, camping on the same farmland outside Frederick that the Rebels had occupied a few days before. On September 13, some Indiana soldiers found three cigars wrapped in a sheet of paper. The cigars were nice, but the real prize was the paper; it was a copy of Lee's confidential orders which revealed how widely he had dispersed his army.

The secret enemy document quickly passed up the chain of command to McClellan. One of McClellan's officers verified its authenticity by recognizing the handwriting of a prewar friend who now served as Lee's adjutant general.

"Here is a paper with which, if I cannot whip Bobby Lee, I will be willing to go home," McClellan boasted. He had, as he wrote Lincoln, "all the plans of the Rebels."

To get at Lee, McClellan marched his army west toward the narrow passes of South Mountain on September 14. There, the outnumbered Confederate defenders bought time with a spirited, day long resistance, allowing Lee to begin gathering his command back together.

Ambrose Burnside and his renowned whiskers. (U.S. Army Military History Institute)

Harpers Ferry surrendered to Jackson on September 15. This success persuaded Lee not to return to Virginia without a fight. The Confederate chieftain ordered his army to reunite in a defensive line along Antietam Creek, near the town of Sharpsburg. It was a bold and even reckless move. The Potomac River ran directly behind the Southern position, effectively eliminating any easy escape should the battle go badly.

All through September 16, the armies sat facing one another: Lee's 40,000 looking at McClellan's 75,000. Then, on September 17, what is traditionally called the bloodiest single day of the Civil War began.

McClellan fought the Battle of Antietam in his usual cautious style, frittering away a numerical advantage by holding troops in reserve and launching uncoordinated offensives. Fighting opened that morning on the western end of the field around a simple, white, Dunkard church. By midday, those troops had fought themselves to a frazzle. The action then shifted toward the center of the lines, where the Unionists tried to storm a Confederate-held sunken road. Forever after it would be known as the Bloody Lane. As the fierce action seesawed back-and-forth, Lee shifted his limited manpower to meet each new threat, using every single one of his reserves.

The Confederates anchored their right flank on heights which overlooked a stone bridge across Antietam Creek. All day long, Union Major General Ambrose Burnside pondered over how best to send his soldiers across the shallow stream. At mid-afternoon, Burnside finally forced a crossing and began to steam-roll the Confederates. Lee had no troops left to stop the onslaught. Disaster loomed.

Then, in the distance, there rose a cloud of dust which indicated the arrival of marching men. As they came into view, blue jackets could be seen, but, a few tense moments later, their flags finally revealed that they were Confederate Major General Ambrose Powell Hill's "Light Division." The last of Jackson's troops to arrive from Harpers Ferry were wearing parts of enemy uniforms which they had captured there.

Hill's timely appearance saved Lee's army. Perhaps it was the memory of this dramatic rescue which caused Hill's name to be uttered by both Lee and Jackson in their final moments of life.

Total casualties for that one day of fighting were nearly 5000 dead, over 18,000 wounded and 3000 missing. Among those tending to the injured soldiers was a 41-year-old, former patent office clerk named Clara Barton. She would become a familiar sight on the battlefields of the Army of the Potomac and, after the war, she would go on to start the American Red Cross.

Ambrose Powell Hill wears three stars in this thoughtful pose.
(U.S. Army Military History Institute)

On September 18, the opposing legions rested in place; McClellan was reluctant to attack and Lee remained unwilling to concede the field. Finally, that evening, the Southerners started back across the Potomac. Their "invasion" had lasted little more than two weeks.

The charge across the Burnside Bridge at Antietam, 1 p.m., September 17th 1862. (Library of Congress)

The Emancipation Proclamation

In mid-summer, Abraham Lincoln showed his cabinet the draft of a document which would free the slaves in the rebellious states. Lincoln's proposal had several intended purposes. First, the promise of freedom would encourage persons of color to come into Union lines and drain the Confederacy of much-needed manual labor. Second, it would serve notice to foreign nations--notably England and France--that support for Confederate independence was, in fact, support for the continuance of slavery. Third, such a proclamation would appease the powerful abolitionist element in the Republican Party and become a first step toward the eventual elimination of the entire system.

Lincoln agreed with his cabinet that, to avoid the appearance of weakness, the proclamation would not be issued until after a military success. Lincoln took Lee's retreat into Virginia, following the stalemate at Antietam, to be that success.

As of January 1, 1863, the Emancipation Proclamation decreed that all slaves in the rebellious states were set free. Of course, Southern plantation owners had other ideas. Nevertheless, word spread among the house servants and field hands that, indeed, the year of jubilee had come and many began slipping away to find Mr. Lincoln's soldiers.

However, slaves in Delaware, Maryland, Kentucky, and Missouri were unaffected as these states had remained in the Union. Not until January 1865 would Congress pass the Thirteenth Amendment to the U.S. Constitution, outlawing the practice of human bondage in the United States.

Thomas Reade Rootes Cobb's first battle experience as a general officer proved to be his last. On December 13, 1862, his brigade held the famous Sunken Road and Stone Wall at Fredericksburg. He exclaimed, "Get ready boys! Here they come!" After the repulse of the Federal assault, a random artillery round sent a piece of metal into the General's left thigh, severing his femoral artery. He died within sight of his mother's childhood home on "Federal Hill." (Sergeant Kirkland's Museum and Historical Society)

Burnside's Fredericksburg Fiasco

Late on the snowy evening of November 7, George McClellan received word that he no longer commanded the Army of the Potomac. Frustrated by McClellan's lack of activity since the fighting at Sharpsburg, Lincoln finally had run out of patience and, in McClellan's stead, he appointed Ambrose Burnside.

This selection came as a curious choice. Even Burnside believed he might not be up to the top job and accepted it only after he was told that, should he refuse, it would be given to another general, "Fighting Joe" Hooker.

When Burnside took command, the Army of the Potomac was cautiously edging its way southeast through northern Virginia. To the south, the First Corps of Lee's Army, under James Longstreet, waited near Culpeper Courthouse. The other half of Lee's force, the Second Corps under Jackson, remained to the west in the Shenandoah Valley.

Burnside decided to make an end run toward Richmond. He ordered his army to move quickly to Fredericksburg. There, a rapid crossing of the Rappahannock River would bring Burnside closer to the Confederate capital than the Rebels.

Burnside won the race. His first troops reached the north shore of the river on November 17, a full day before any of Longstreet's men. However, following Burnside's orders, the Federals halted and waited for the arrival of pontoon boats. Not until December 11 did Burnside finally begin bridging the Rappahannock.

That delay gave Lee time to place his whole army on the heights just south of Fredericksburg. Though their numbers were only two-thirds that of the bluecoats, the well-protected Confederate position dominated an open field that their enemies had to cross.

Using the houses of Fredericksburg for cover, Mississippi riflemen took deadly aim on the Union engineers attempting to put the pontoon bridges in place. When the Yankees got across the river, they exacted their revenge by sacking the historic old town.

On the foggy morning of December 13, the Northerners began a series of gallant, but foolhardy, attacks on the Confederate line. Wearing their sky-blue winter overcoats, they rushed forward and were slaughtered. Of an estimated 120,000 going into the fight, 12,700 became casualties. The Rebels lost only 5300.

This photograph was taken from the Union-held Falmouth side of the Rappahannock River looking at a Confederate officer and his men on the Confederate held Fredericksburg side. Just a few months prior, the railroad-bridge was blown up after the Yankees fled this southern town. The house on the hill and Confederate earthworks, in the distance stood atop Willis' Hill, later known as Mayre's Heights. (Library of Congress)

At the end of the day, Burnside wanted to personally lead one last doomed charge. His subordinates talked him out of it. That night, from the frozen no-man's land between the two armies, the pitiful cries of the blueclad wounded rang out into the December darkness.

By morning, Sergeant Richard Rowland Kirkland, a 19-year-old South Carolinian, could stand their misery no longer. He took several canteens and, for over an hour, left the safety of the Confederate line to aid his enemies. The watching Federal army held its fire while they cheered his humanitarian efforts. Kirkland, nevertheless, did not survive the war; he died a year later at the Battle of Chickamauga.

On the 14th, Burnside considered renewing his attack but recognized the futility of it. Instead, he took his army back to camp on the north bank of the Rappahannock.

Burnside attempted a new campaign in January; this, however, quickly turned into a wintertime mud march and the move was abandoned. On January 25, Lincoln removed the unfortunate general from command and "Fighting Joe" Hooker took charge.

Veterans of the western army, the 21st Michigan Infantry fought at Stones River and Chickamauga. (U.S. Army Military History Institute)

General Bragg Invades Kentucky

At the same time Robert E. Lee marched into Maryland, General Braxton Bragg led his Army of the Tennessee into Kentucky. Bragg had risen to the command of the western army when General Beauregard left to recuperate from illness after the fall of Corinth.

Bragg, a West Point graduate, had served as an officer in the old army before resigning to become a Louisiana planter. He held the confidence of Jefferson Davis, an essential credential for anyone hoping to succeed in the Confederate high command.

Unfortunately, Bragg's considerable military skills suffered in comparison to his prickly personality. There is a famous story of Bragg serving as both company commander and quartermaster at an army post before the war. As company commander, he requested supplies. As quartermaster, he denied the request. Finally, he referred the matter to a surprised superior who exclaimed, "You have quarreled with every officer in the army and now you are quarreling with yourself!"

Bragg's tenure as army commander would be marked by the near-mutiny of his subordinates and growing hostility among the rank and file; the consequences would be severe for the future of the Confederacy. But the first part of his Kentucky invasion was nothing less than brilliant.

After the fall of Corinth, Grant guarded the gains made in western Tennessee and made preparations for a future campaign against the Rebel stronghold of Vicksburg, Mississippi. Buell, whose arrival at Shiloh helped save the day for Grant, turned toward Chattanooga, another vital rail center and gateway to Georgia.

But Bragg did not sit idly by. Near the end of summer, he seized the initiative. Leaving behind a small force under Major General Earl Van Dorn to watch Grant, the Army of the Tennessee took an extended train trip through the heart of Dixie, traveling to Chattanooga by way of Mobile. The roundabout journey was required as the Yankees controlled the direct rail route.

Reaching Chattanooga, Bragg's brave boys flanked around Buell's Yankees and made an end run to Kentucky. Other Confederates commanded by Major General Kirby Smith marched out of Knoxville, also bound for the bluegrass state.

Buell had no choice but to follow. Without fighting a battle, Bragg made the enemy retreat two hundred miles in a foot race to see who could reach Louisville first. The capture of this city would put the Rebels on the road to invade the Midwest and could improve significantly the prospects of peace candidates in the North's mid-term elections.

On September 18, one day after the Battle of Antietam, the Confederates stood poised to capture Louisville. Panic reigned in the poorly defended city, but Bragg did not know how strong its defenses were and, in any event, he expected he could not hold onto the place for very long. He decided to forego the prize. His troops turned east.

It was at that point that Bragg's brilliant campaign began to falter. The Confederate commander left his army and went off to arrange for the inauguration of a Confederate governor at the state capitol in Frankfort. This attempt to give legitimacy to a Confederate Kentucky was short-lived; the new governor left office when Bragg's men left the state.

Buell's bluecoats encountered the Rebels just outside the little town of Perryville on October 8. Bragg had failed to concentrate Confederate strength and none of Kirby Smith's men were present. As a consequence, the greybacks were badly outnumbered; even worse, Bragg did not realize that most of the Union army was present. He ordered an aggressive attack against the Federal left.

In savage fighting, the Confederates drove the Unionists from that part of the field. However, in the Yankee center stood the division of 31-year-old Phil Sheridan, who had just received his general's star. "Little Phil" was determined to prove himself worthy. His troops held their ground against the enemy attack and the day ended in a stalemate. The Confederates, though, had narrowly escaped disaster; only nine of the twenty-four Union brigades were heavily engaged in the battle. An entire Federal corps had remained inactive, even though it was in position to envelop the Confederate flank.

Recognizing the danger, Bragg withdrew from the field and then from the state, taking his troops all the way back to Tennessee. It was the first of many times the general was to bring disappointment and controversy to his army. Jefferson Davis summoned him to Richmond to explain the retreat, but Bragg successfully placated the president and managed to remain in command.

Buell, though, did not fare as well. Dissatisfied that Bragg was both allowed to enter and escape from Kentucky, Lincoln removed Buell and named Major General William Rosecrans to lead the Army of the Cumberland.

West Pointer Rosecrans had come fresh from a victory over Earl Van Dorn when the Confederates had tried to retake Corinth, Mississippi, at the beginning of October. Rosecrans reorganized his new command in Nashville as he made plans for a campaign against Chattanooga.

Bragg, meanwhile, moved the Army of the Tennessee to a line only thirty-one miles from Nashville, along Stones River, near the town of

Murfreesboro. Rosecrans moved out to meet Bragg on the day after Christmas, 1862. Rebel cavalry slowed Rosecrans' advance but, on the last day of the year, the battle began.

Rosecrans intended to attack Bragg; however, Bragg struck first and scattered the far right of the Union army. As at Perryville, the blue center maintained order, although they were forced to withdraw to another position in order to protect their flank. Bragg continued to attack the new Union line but failed to break through it.

Nevertheless, despite heavy losses, he felt confident that his army had won a victory, and he telegraphed Jefferson Davis that "God has granted us a happy new year."

Contrary to Bragg's expectations, Rosecrans' Yankees did not quit the field that evening. The two armies quietly faced each other through a cheerless New Year's Day, 1863.

The lull continued into January 2 until four p.m., when Bragg ordered Major General John Breckinridge to attack four brigades that were isolated from the Union left by the icy waters of Stones River. Breckinridge, a former vice president of the United States, protested that Union artillery across the river would smash the assault. Bragg repeated his order and Breckinridge's Kentuckians proceeded to drive the enemy across Stones River. Then fifty-eight massed Federal cannons opened up on Breckinridge and fresh Union troops knocked him back to his starting point. The assault--and its casualties--had been in vain.

Some of Bragg's subordinates counseled retreat. Bragg, at first, refused and then he agreed. Rosecrans' men held the field and, accordingly, could claim bragging rights that the inconclusive and bloody contest was a Northern victory.

As it had after Perryville, dissension over the debacle divided the top officers of the Army of the Tennessee. It did not bode well for the army's future success.

1863

The Grey Ghost

In the wee hours of March 9, 1863, a small band of Confederate raiders slipped through Union lines and into Fairfax Courthouse, just outside Washington, D.C. Their leader, a lawyer-turned-warrior named John Singleton Mosby, stole into the bedroom of Brigadier General Edwin Stoughton, who was sleeping off the effects of a party he had attended earlier. Mosby tossed up the Union officer's nightshirt, slapped his rump and said, "General, have you ever heard of Mosby?"

The shocked Stoughton stammered, "Yes! Have you caught him?"

"No," Mosby replied, "he has caught you."

Such exploits made Mosby and his men legendary throughout the wartime South. A section of northern Virginia became known as Mosby's Confederacy and the slight 125-pound raider's word ruled as law.

Mosby had a hair-trigger temper. As a student at the University of Virginia, he shot a man who had threatened him and subsequently served a term in prison where he decided to become a lawyer. A Unionist until Virginia seceded, he enlisted as a private in the First Virginia Cavalry before going on to serve as a scout for J.E.B. Stuart.

In January 1863, Mosby began his career as a partisan. Through the end of the war, he and his rangers disrupted Union supply lines, attacked enemy picket posts and generally made life miserable for the Northern invaders. In October 1864, they derailed a Baltimore-and-Ohio passenger train, capturing a Union payroll of $173,000, which was divided among the raiders. As was his custom, Mosby accepted none of the loot, though his men took up a collection and purchased a fine horse which they gave to their commander.

Union efforts failed numerous times to eliminate the guerrillas, and the end of the conflict found Mosby as a full colonel in charge of some eight hundred men. Rather than surrender, he disbanded his command.

Though often wounded during the war, Mosby lived on until 1916, returning to the practice of law and serving as U.S. Consul to Hong Kong. He also became friends with President U.S. Grant, who had once advised his soldiers to hang Mosby's raiders without trial.

Interestingly, John Mosby is the Confederate officer most often mentioned in Robert E. Lee's wartime papers. Some historians argue his activities extended the life of the Confederacy by as much as six months.

Joseph Hooker, befuddled at Chancellorsville. (U.S. Army Military History Institute)

Chancellorsville:
Stonewall's Final Fight

"May God have mercy on General Lee for I shall have none," declared Major General Joseph Hooker as he began the Army of Potomac's latest campaign to capture Richmond. The general's nickname, "Fighting Joe," came about as a result of a newspaper report which read: "still fighting Joe Hooker."

The nickname stuck as did rumors of weakness where women and liquor were concerned. However, Hooker did swear off alcohol upon accepting command of the army, although, in retrospect, he might have done a better job had he had an occasional nip. Also, for the record, there is no truth to the story that Hooker's name is the origin of the slang term for prostitute; ladies of the evening were called "hookers" long before the general rose to fame.

That winter, Hooker had overseen the reorganization of the Army of the Potomac into a splendid combat force of 134,000. "The finest army on the planet," he boasted. Hooker used part of that army to hold Lee in position at Fredericksburg, while the bulk of the blue troops moved several miles to the west and forded the Rappahannock River. This put Hooker on Lee's left flank and in position to get between the Confederates and Richmond.

For once, the bluecoats had gotten a jump on Lee. What's more, only a part of Lee's army was present; Longstreet had not returned from southeastern Virginia where his men had been gathering supplies and engaging in an unsuccessful effort to recapture Suffolk . To face Hooker's mighty hordes, the Rebels could rally only 60,000 soldiers.

Ever the gambler, Lee resorted to his usual and necessary strategy of dividing the army. He left Major General Jubal Early with 10,000 troops in the trenches behind Fredericksburg; they would oppose the 40,000 Yankees under Major General John Sedgwick who had crossed the Rappahannock there. Meanwhile, Lee and Jackson took the remainder of the army to handle Hooker.

For once, "Fighting Joe" didn't seem to feel like fighting. Instead of advancing rapidly toward Richmond, he surrendered the initiative and pulled his troops into the heavily wooded terrain around the crossroads of Chancellorsville. Here his overwhelming numbers counted for less than had he continued southward to open country.

The last photo of "Stonewall" Jackson, taken in the spring of 1863, just before his mortal wounding at Chancellorsville. (Library of Congress)

Jackson discovered that Hooker's right flank was exposed and vulnerable to attack. He proposed to Lee that the army yet again be divided, allowing "Stonewall" to take the bulk of the troops on a 14-mile flank march to launch a surprise attack on the enemy. In the meantime, Lee would have just two divisions to hold back the bulk of blue invaders.

Lee agreed and demonstrated noisily with his few remaining men, successfully diverting Hooker's attention while Jackson circled around the enemy line. Word of the Confederate march did get back to Hooker, and he decided that Lee was retreating to escape certain destruction.

On the evening of May 2, Jackson attacked and routed the exposed right flank of the Union line. Northern soldiers, who had been peacefully preparing an evening meal just a few minutes before, ran for their lives. Only darkness halted the Confederate success.

It was a hellish night in those tangled woods. Both armies were nervous and jumpy. While planning for the renewal of his attack, Jackson and some aides went to scout the Union position. They ended up between the two lines and, in the uncertain darkness, they were mistaken for Union cavalry. Shots from a North Carolina unit mortally wounded "Stonewall" Jackson, and the devoutly religious soldier passed into eternity on May 10. He died on a Sunday and that pleased him.

The loss of Jackson was immeasurable, but Lee still had Hooker's army to push back across the river. Cavalry commander J.E.B. Stuart temporarily took charge of Jackson's men, and the next day consisted of punishing assaults against the reformed Union line.

A Confederate cannon shot crashed into a column on the porch of Hooker's headquarters and nearly killed the commanding general. He survived, dazed but basically unharmed. Nevertheless, most of the fight had been knocked out of "Fighting Joe." By nightfall, the Union army withdrew to yet another position, closer to the Rappahannock River.

However, a more pressing problem now occupied Lee. Sedgwick's Yankees had pushed Early's outnumbered Confederates out of their old trenches at Fredericksburg. Sedgwick was quickly coming up behind Lee's command and Lee dispatched more troops to drive Sedgwick away. Only 25,000 Confederates remained behind to hold Hooker's 90,000 at bay.

But the move worked. Sedgwick was defeated at Salem Church and forced back across the Rappahannock River.

Hooker also decided to call it quits and, over the objections of several subordinates, ordered a general retreat. Joe Hooker was whipped even if his army was not; many of his soldiers had not even seen any fighting.

When news of the Union defeat reached Washington, Lincoln reacted with despair. "My God! What will the country say?" he asked.

Hundreds of Southern women took to the streets of Richmond in April 1863, to protest high prices and food shortages. A few months later, the North would be shocked by the draft riots in New York City. (Frank Leslie's Illustrated Newspaper, May 23, 1863)

Gettysburg:
Lee's Second Invasion of the North

With the death of "Stonewall" Jackson, Lee reorganized his army in three corps: the First, commanded by his "old war horse," James Longstreet; the Second, commanded by Richard Ewell, who had recently returned to service after losing a leg in the Second Manassas Campaign; and the Third, commanded by Ambrose Powell Hill, whose timely arrival had saved the army at Sharpsburg.

Lee again pinned his hopes on an invasion of the North. Ewell's Corps led the way, marching into the Shenandoah Valley where the Blue Ridge would screen the move from Hooker.

As the Rebel advance got underway, Federal horsemen splashed across the Rappahannock River and surprised J.E.B. Stuart's troops at Brandy Station. Stuart's headquarters was overrun but, at the end of the day, he still held the field, and so the largest cavalry battle in North American history is recorded as a Southern victory. It was proof, however, that the Federal mounted troops were becoming an equal match for their Confederate counterparts.

Ewell reached Winchester on June 14 where he won a substantial victory over Major General Robert Milroy. This cleared the way north. Ewell swept through Maryland and into Pennsylvania, followed by Hill and Longstreet.

Lee's men ranged across south-central Pennsylvania on a broad front, gathering supplies and generally enjoying themselves as much as soldiers can in wartime. They came within a few miles of capturing Harrisburg, Pennsylvania's capital, but Lee recalled his troops as he had learned Hooker's army was in pursuit.

Actually, it was no longer Hooker's army. Lincoln had grown weary with the failures of "Fighting Joe" and, when Hooker requested to be relieved of command due to a dispute over troops at Harpers Ferry, Lincoln called his bluff and agreed to do so.

Thus rose George Gordon Meade, a professional soldier from a Philadelphia family. Meade had a solid record of service in the war, though he was far from being a charismatic leader. His receding hairline, grizzled beard and gaunt appearance made him look older than his 48-years, and he was given to occasional outbursts of crankiness.

Meade received word of his promotion just three days before the fighting opened at Gettysburg on July 1. It is one of the ironies of history that he is today less remembered than Robert E. Lee, the man he defeated.

Major General George Gordon Meade, commander of the Army of the Potomac. (National Archives)

Newspaper illustrator Alfred Waud was an eyewitness to the fighting on Seminary Ridge, where troops from A.P. Hill's III Corps broke the Union line and sent the Federals fleeing late in the afternoon of July 1. (National Archives)

Gettysburg, Pennsylvania, where the armies collided, was a little crossroads courthouse town. Legend has it that the Confederates were looking for shoes. It's just as likely they were looking for a fight, despite Lee's desire not to bring on a general engagement until his army was concentrated. In war, as in life, things sometimes just happen.

In fact, on the first day, events could not have gone much better for the Rebels even if they had been carefully planned. What began as a skirmish west of the town quickly grew into a hard-fought battle as more and more troops reached the field. Union Major General John Reynolds, an outstanding corps commander who had turned down Lincoln's offer to lead the army, died from a Confederate bullet early in the fight. Nevertheless, the Union soldiers held their own until mid-afternoon when Jubal Early's greybacks arrived and attacked the North's right flank. About the same time, the Confederates also hit the Union left and soon bluecoats dashed in disorder through the streets of Gettysburg.

The Federal retreat stopped just south of town on Cemetery Hill. This became the anchor of a new position which, when reinforcements arrived, took the shape of a fishhook. As dusk fell, the Confederates failed to follow-up their advantage with a final assault on the new Union line. To this day, historians argue what the results would have been if they had done so.

Through most of July 2, more men from both armies reached the battlefield. In late afternoon, Longstreet attacked the Union left. The bluecoats narrowly beat back an effort to capture Little Round Top, whose heights overlooked the entire Union position. Confederate offensives along other parts of the Union line were also ferocious but failed to achieve a breakthrough.

Armistead's brigade — the 9th, 14th, 38th 53rd, and 57th, Virginia — occupied the left of Pickett's line. Lewis Addison Armistead fell at the high water mark of the Confederacy. (Library of Congress)

On Friday, July 3, confident of the abilities of his soldiers, Lee decided to gamble. After an awesome early afternoon artillery duel, he sent approximately 13,000 men across an open field to smash the Federal center on Cemetery Ridge three-quarters of a mile away. This has become popularly known as "Pickett's Charge," although the ringlet-haired major general, George Pickett, commanded only a portion of the troops involved.

As drums rolled and flags waved, the brave Confederates marched with shouldered muskets and fixed bayonets toward their former countrymen, the enemy. Forever after in history, this afternoon would symbolize the high tide of Southern hopes.

But it was not to be. Such an assault, more suited to the era of Napoleon than the age of rifled muskets and cannon, was hopeless from the start. Yankee gunfire decimated the grey ranks. Some Confederates managed to reach the Union line, but they were soon killed, captured or forced to flee.

As the survivors of the charge returned, Lee rode forward to meet them, saying that it was alright, and that the failure was his fault. Spying General Pickett, Lee ordered him to gather his division and prepare to defend against any Union counterattack. Pickett emotionally replied, "General Lee, I have no division now."

Lee held his army in place for one more day, buying time for a 17-mile long wagon train of wounded to wend its way back to Virginia. Total casualties--killed, wounded and captured--for both sides stood somewhere around 50,000.

Meade's careful and correct pursuit of the defeated but still dangerous Rebels drew criticism from many, including President Lincoln. Regardless, the fact remained that Lee was driven from Pennsylvania and he would never lead his army there again.

Through the remainder of 1863, the eastern antagonists recovered from their losses and engaged in two inconclusive campaigns, Bristoe Station and Mine Run. Then the two armies settled into winter camps near Culpeper, Virginia, to await the coming of spring and a continuation of the carnage.

The legendary Daniel Edgar Sickles. (U.S. Army Military History Institute)

The Colorful General Sickles

In 1859, Congressman Dan Sickles shot and killed his wife's lover, the son of "Star Spangled Banner" author Francis Scott Key, in Lafayette Square, just across from the White House. Defended by Attorney Edwin Stanton, later Lincoln's secretary of war, Sickles won acquittal by pleading temporary insanity. Many Victorian minds, however, felt that the real scandal came when the cuckolded husband forgave his wife and accepted her back into his home! As a coda to the whole affair, Mrs. Sickles committed suicide.

When the war began, Sickles received a brigadier general's commission and raised a brigade of New York troops. Unlike many political generals, Sickles showed some actual ability and he rose to corps command. At Chancellorsville, his troops attacked "Stonewall" Jackson while he was making his flank march, but Sickles failed to stop Jackson or understand the true intent of the enemy movement.

Two months later, on the second day at Gettysburg, the Chancellorsville experience convinced Sickles that the Union army was again being flanked, this time by Longstreet. Without orders, Sickles marched his troops out of position to meet the Rebels. It came close to being a disaster and Sickles' corps suffered heavy losses. However, Longstreet's attack was blunted.

Dan Sickles was among the casualties. Puffing on a cigar, he was carried from the field with a badly mangled right leg which was later amputated.

Sickles recovered from his wound to go on to more adventures in what was a full and active life. He went abroad as minister to Spain and served again in Congress. He also played a key role in the development of the national military park at Gettysburg.

As for his leg, the old general gave it to the national medical museum in Washington where he frequently visited it until his death in 1914.

Lincoln's Gettysburg Address

As the only major battle fought above the Mason-Dixon line, Gettysburg drew much attention and received many visitors from the North. While the killed Confederate were buried expeditiously in mass graves, a national cemetery was created for the Union dead. On November 19, 1863, Abraham Lincoln came to the dedication ceremonies and gave this two-minute speech.

Four score and seven years ago, our fathers brought forth on this continent a new nation, conceived in liberty and dedicated to the proposition that all men are created equal.

Now we are engaged in a great civil war, testing whether that nation, or any nation so conceived and so dedicated, can long endure. We are met on a great battlefield of that war. We have come to dedicate a portion of that field as a final resting place for those who here gave their lives that that nation might live. It is altogether fitting and proper that we should do this.

But, in a larger sense, we cannot dedicate, we cannot consecrate, we cannot hallow this ground. The brave men, living and dead, who struggled here, have consecrated it far above our poor power to add or detract. The world will little note, nor long remember, what we say here, but it can never forget what they did here. It is for us the living, rather, to be dedicated here to the unfinished work which they who fought here have thus far so nobly advanced. It is rather for us to be here dedicated to the great work remaining before us -- that from these honored dead, we take increased devotion to the cause for which they gave the last full measure of devotion--that we here highly resolve that these dead shall not have died in vain--that this nation, under God, shall have a new birth of freedom--and that government of the people, by the people, for the people, shall not perish from the earth.

The best known of Nathan Bedford Forrest's several wartime portraits, and probably made in mid-1864. (U.S. Army Military History Institute)

General Braxton Bragg's prickly personality made him unpopular among his subordinates and his troops. Nathan Bedford Forrest called him a "damned scoundrel." (Sergeant Kirkland's Museum and Historical Society)

Vicksburg:
Key to the Mississippi

Since the fighting at Shiloh in April 1862, U.S. Grant had had a frustrating time of it. Appointed in October 1862 as commander of the Department of the Tennessee, Grant tried to advance southward through Mississippi to capture the Confederate stronghold of Vicksburg.

The overland route proved to be a mistake, however, as Rebel horsemen under Nathan Bedford Forrest and Earl Van Dorn played havoc with the Union supply lines. When Van Dorn destroyed more than $1.5 million worth of Federal food and equipment at Holly Springs, Mississippi, in December, Grant acknowledged his error and returned to Tennessee. Nevertheless, with the characteristic determination that marked his military career, he did not give up the idea of capturing Vicksburg.

Vicksburg was important because, coupled with the fortifications at Port Hudson, Louisiana, it guarded the last 150-mile stretch of the mighty Mississippi River not under Union control. Seizing Vicksburg would slice the Confederacy in two, isolating Texas and the rest of the trans-Mississippi region. It would also deprive the eastern Confederacy of supplies that were skirting the blockade by being shipped into Mexico and carried across the Rio Grande.

Jefferson Davis, whose plantation home lay not far from the strategic city, responded to the Yankee threat with an awkward command structure which would greatly assist the Union army in achieving its goal.

In charge at Vicksburg was Lieutenant General John C. Pemberton, a Pennsylvania-born Mexican War hero who had married a Virginia woman and cast his lot with the South. Joe Johnston, freshly returned to duty after recuperating from his wound received at Seven Pines, now headed the overwhelmingly large Department of the West. He served as Pemberton's immediate superior.

But Johnston felt that his was more of a titular role since he lacked direct command of an actual army. What's more, he frequently found his ideas were in conflict with those of President Davis. He also was unhappy that upon his recovery he had not been returned to lead the Army of Northern Virginia.

The Confederate strength lay in geography. Vicksburg had the attributes of a natural fortress. Approaches from the west faced the obstacle of the Mississippi River with strong batteries of Confederate artillery well positioned to punish any unwelcome visitors. To the north, swamps and bayous blocked the invaders' path as Major General William Sherman discovered when the Confederates beat him back at Chickasaw Bluffs in December. Grant had already tried and failed in taking the easterly overland route to the city. Somehow he needed to get his army south of Vicksburg where more open country would give him room to campaign.

At the end of March 1863, Grant's men began building a military road down the west bank of the Mississippi River. This would allow them to safely bypass Vicksburg and cross the waterway below the city. Sherman continued to pressure the Rebels from the north.

To ferry his troops across the Mississippi, Grant needed the ships of the Union navy. They would have to run the gantlet of the Vicksburg guns. On the night of April 16, Admiral David Porter sailed a blue flotilla of twelve vessels downstream through an explosive hail of Rebel shot and shell. Only one ship fell victim to the bombardment. Two weeks later, Grant's army safely crossed to the east bank of the river.

Taking another risk, Grant cut loose from his tenuous supply line and marched toward Jackson, Mississippi's state capital and Vicksburg's sole rail link to the outside world. There Joe Johnston and 12,000 grey soldiers retreated in the face of Grant's 20,000 bluecoats. The Northern commander slept in the hotel room which the Southern general had occupied the night before.

Grant's adroit action skillfully placed his army between the two smaller enemy forces. Aided by confidential Confederate correspondence captured by an undercover courier, Grant quickly turned to beat Pemberton who had hesitantly left Vicksburg's defenses in hope of joining Johnston.

Throughout the campaign, Pemberton was confused. Given a Yankee army that seemed to be moving in all directions, it was difficult to discern the invader's true intentions. Beyond that, his two superiors sent conflicting orders; President Davis urged him to "hold Vicksburg at all hazard" while Johnston instructed him to march east so they could coordinate their attacks against the enemy.

On May 16, Grant's army defeated Pemberton's outnumbered men at Champion Hill. In the retreat, one of the Confederate divisions got lost and eventually wandered its way into Johnston's camp, but the remainder of Pemberton's people pulled back to the defenses of Vicksburg.

Joe Johnston sent word to abandon the city. Pemberton felt that moving his men and material might be impossible. Besides that, he had direct orders from the president to stay put.

Confident with their success so far, the Yankees tried and failed to storm the Vicksburg fortifications on May 19 and 22. For several days afterward, blue wounded suffered in the no-man's land between the lines because Grant refused to request a truce to remove them. Finally, on May 25, Pemberton ended the agony by asking Grant to get his injured off the field.

The shooting settled into a siege, and Union artillery on land and water belched tons of iron into the surrounded city. Confederate guns defiantly boomed back though each answer shrank their limited supply of shot and shell. Grant had no such concerns for his communication lines with the North were again secure, and his army was growing stronger in both soldiers and supplies.

For almost seven weeks, the ring tightened around Vicksburg. Residents dug caves into hillsides to escape the enemy bombardment and, as foodstuffs disappeared, some dined on mule and rat.

At the end, the inhabitants lived mainly on the hope that Joe Johnston could come to their rescue, but Johnston didn't have the manpower to go against the Yankees on his own. On July 3, Pemberton met Grant between the lines to talk terms, and the next day he surrendered his 29,000 men.

Coming immediately after the Union triumph at Gettysburg, it was a happy Fourth of July for the North. Port Hudson fell a few days later. The Union forces then controlled the entire length of the Mississippi River, and the Confederacy sat split in two. As Abraham Lincoln said, "the father of the waters now flows unvexed to the sea."

Following the capture of Vicksburg, Confederate forces west of the river were pretty much on their own. The vast trans-Mississippi was nicknamed "Kirby Smithdom," after the commanding general. Smith's forces became so isolated from Richmond that war department orders often seemed irrelevant. Nevertheless, they fought on alone and did not give up until June 2, 1865, nearly two months after the surrender of Robert E. Lee.

Grant's Headquarters at Vicksburg

A Wild Rebel Raid Through the Midwest

In two years of war, John Hunt Morgan had made a name for himself as one of the true cavaliers of the Confederacy. His raids across Tennessee and his native Kentucky exasperated enemy commanders and made Morgan legend down in Dixie.

But his biggest exploit came in July 1863. Disobeying orders to remain south of the Ohio River, Morgan led his hell-for-leather riders on an amazing and somewhat foolhardy 25-day foray across southern Indiana and Ohio. Coming at the same time as Lee's invasion into Pennsylvania, the raiders ran riot across the Midwest, spreading panic and, for a time, making fools of their pursuers.

Along the 700-mile route, Morgan captured and paroled some six thousand Yankees while destroying railroads, bridges and other property. Reaching eastern Ohio, a portion of his command crossed back over the Ohio River to safety; however, Union pursuit made it impossible for all to escape so Morgan stayed behind with the remainder of his men. The madcap adventure continued on.

Exhausted and nearly out of ammunition, the weary grey general knew that capture was inevitable. Hoping to gain better terms, he surrendered to a surprised militia officer whom he had already taken prisoner. The long wild ride finally came to an end not far from the Pennsylvania border.

Morgan's surrender ploy failed to gain him any advantage. He and his officers were carted off to Columbus and imprisoned in the Ohio Penitentiary, where their heads were shaved in the style of common convicts.

The Kentuckian, though, could not be held for very long. That November, he and several of his men tunneled to freedom and escaped back to the South. A year later, the grey cavalier's career came to a deadly conclusion. Yankee cavalry surprised and killed the general during an early morning raid in Greeneville, Tennessee.

After the sacking, burning, and slaughter at Lawrence, Kansas, by William Quantrill's Confederate guerrillas on August 21, 1863, Northern newspapers such as the Chicago Tribune branded them all "fiends incarnate." (Sergeant Kirkland's Museum and Historical Society)

The Sacking of Lawrence, Kansas

Along the Kansas and Missouri border, much of the Civil War was simply a continuation of the carnage that had racked the region in the 1850's. Abolitionist bands called "jayhawkers" traded atrocities with pro-Southern bushwhackers much as they did during the "Bleeding Kansas" period, except now the enlarged hostilities were formally sanctioned as war.

It was up-close and personal fighting, neighbor against neighbor. Outrages were commonplace. The harsh aspects of frontier survival seemed to give license to a brutality far beyond that of the eastern armies.

One of the most feared bands of raiders was led by William Clarke Quantrill, an Ohio native with a curious history. In the years before the conflict officially began, Quantrill had joined the jayhawkers in battling the slaveholders. But he fell out of favor with the free-staters, due to his flair for indiscriminate thievery. Quantrill changed sides by leading several of his former comrades into a trap.

During the war, Quantrill wrangled a Confederate captain's commission and raised a troop which included men who would become some America's most famous outlaws. Jesse James, Frank James, "Bloody Bill" Anderson and Cole Younger all rode with him.

On August 21, 1863, Quantrill's men committed their most infamous act. At dawn, the desperados--four hundred strong-- approached Lawrence, Kansas, a well-known abolitionist stronghold and, not coincidentally, Quantrill's old stomping ground.

The attack, at least in part, was intended as revenge. Union forces had made hostages of some women whose men-folk were in Quantrill's band. Tragically, the building in Kansas City where the ladies were imprisoned had collapsed, killing and injuring several of them. What's more, a just-issued Federal directive, Order Number Ten, instructed that all families of known guerrillas would be forcibly moved out of Missouri.

So the raiders were in an angry mood as they thundered their horses through the streets of Lawrence. They shot any man they saw. A small detachment of Union recruits was scattered and most were killed.

While Quantrill ate breakfast at the Eldridge Hotel, his cutthroats began a four-hour rampage of plunder, murder and arson. Following their leader's instructions, any man big enough to carry a gun was slaughtered--some 150 in all.

However, a particular target did escape; Jim Lane, a U.S. Senator who had earned his own violent reputation in the border fighting, avoided capture by hiding in a cornfield. Quantrill wanted to take Lane back to Missouri for a public execution.

As the town went up in flames, Quantrill's men made their get-away. One raider, too drunk to mount his horse, was dragged around Lawrence by the enraged survivors and then stoned to death.

Quantrill himself survived until the very end of the war. Union pressure forced him to flee to Kentucky and there, on May 10, 1865, he was gunned down in a barnyard. Paralyzed by a pistol ball in his spine, Quantrill went as a Union prisoner to Louisville, where he died June 6.

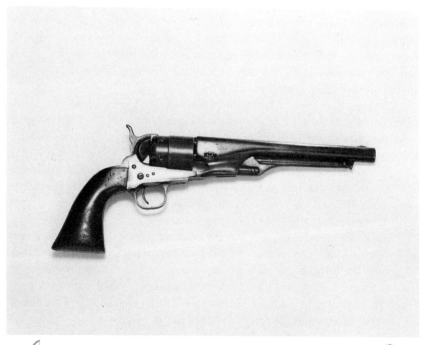

The war's most popular revolver, the 44-caliber Army Colt. (Author's Collection. Photo by Brenda Goodhart.)

Chickamauga: River of Death

Following the battle at Stones River, the vital rail center of Chattanooga became the prize which Rosecrans' Yankees hoped to capture and Bragg's Confederates had to hold. But, for half a year, Rosecrans rested in place near Murfreesboro, recovering from the New Year's fighting and securing his position. The Union commander curiously rationalized that any successful forward movement by his army might result in Bragg sending troops to embattled Vicksburg!

Bragg, for his part, made good use of the long reprieve from combat. Rations were scarce in the Confederacy and that year's winter wheat crop promised to be a record setter. Soldiers from the Army of the Tennessee were dispatched to help in the harvest.

Union movement toward the gateway city of Chattanooga finally began in the summer of 1863. Rosecrans' skillful maneuvering forced Bragg's army out of middle Tennessee without a fight.

In early September, Rosecrans deceived Bragg into thinking the blue army would cross the Tennessee River north of Chattanooga when, in fact, the bulk of it crossed to the south. Outflanked, Bragg evacuated the city on September 6.

So far so good for the Federals. But the war department urged continued aggressive action, and Rosecrans moved his troops through the mountains into Georgia without pausing to concentrate them. Confederate deserters encouraged the Yankees' advance, telling tales of panic and dismay in Bragg's army.

The deserters, however, had been planted by Bragg to spread such stories; in reality, the Rebels eagerly waited to pounce upon the separated enemy columns. Here was one of the South's golden opportunities to destroy a Federal army and possibly reverse the course of the war. But it was not to be. Bragg's plans failed as his senior commanders bungled the job, not once but twice. Alerted to the danger, Rosecrans urgently tried to bring his army together.

On September 19, the opposing forces met south of the Tennessee state line near Chickamauga Creek, a Cherokee Indian name meaning "River of Death." Rosecrans had some 58,000 men while Bragg actually outnumbered him with 66,000. Reinforcements from Virginia--part of Longstreet's Corps from Lee's army--were just arriving after a tiring trip on the South's ramshackle rail system.

On the evening of September 19, Confederate Major General Patrick Cleburne's column fanned out in a line that stretched for a half a mile and attacked the Federal divisions commanded by Brigadier Generals Richard Johnson and Absolom Baird. (Library of Congress)

The first day's fighting ended inconclusively as the Confederates failed in their attempts to cut off the enemy from Chattanooga. Bragg ordered more assaults the next day. These, too, accomplished little except to kill more men. Then fate intervened.

In the thick woodlands, a Union officer believed he saw a gap in the Federal line. Alerted to this, Rosecrans ordered a division moved to fill in the hole. In reality, no gap existed but Rosecrans' order created one at the very moment that Longstreet's men punched into that part of the line. Sixteen thousand Confederates broke through, taking three dozen artillery pieces and routing most of four Union divisions. Fortune, which had so often frowned upon the Army of Tennessee, decided on this day to smile. Much of the Union army, including their commander, fled back toward Chattanooga in disorder. But about half of the Northerners, under the command of Major General George Thomas, stayed behind to fight.

Thomas was a professional soldier and a Virginian who refused to follow his native state out of the Union; instead, he remained in the national army. Learning of this decision, his family had turned his portrait to face the wall and never spoke of him again. Throughout the war, "Old Pap" compiled a steady record of service and, on this day, he won lasting renown as the "Rock of Chickamauga."

With the Union right disintegrating, Thomas drew his men into a defensive position on Snodgrass Hill. He told them that they must hold there or die. From mid-afternoon until dusk, they endured repeated poundings from the enemy. Finally those bluecoats still living were allowed to follow their comrades in retreat. The fierce resistance of Thomas' men had saved the army from destruction.

Chickamauga gave Braxton Bragg and the Army of the Tennessee their greatest triumph. Characteristically, Bragg failed to follow this advantage with a determined pursuit of a beaten foe. Rosecrans took his troops back into Chattanooga and began fortifying the city. Bragg followed with the idea that a siege would starve the Yankees into submission.

Chattanooga:
Battle Above the Clouds

Despite the Confederate victory, there was little happiness among the Army of the Tennessee's high command following Chickamauga. Ensconced above Chattanooga on the heights of Lookout Mountain and Missionary Ridge, the Rebels had trapped the enemy in the city and successfully cut most of their communications to the outside world. It seemed there was little to do but wait for Rosecrans to starve or surrender. This gave the Rebel leaders time for their favorite intramural activity, quarreling over the last battle.

The situation grew so tense that eleven of the army's generals, including the recently arrived Longstreet, sent a petition to President Davis urging the removal of Braxton Bragg. The president hurried to the army and proceeded to paper over its problems by demoting or replacing most of those opposed to Bragg.

About this time, Nathan Bedford Forrest, never a shrinking violet, entered Bragg's tent and delivered an ear-scorching tirade. "If you were any part of a man, I would slap your jaws and force you to resent it," Forrest thundered, calling the commander a "damned scoundrel." He warned that if Bragg ever tried to interfere with him again it would be at the peril of his life. Too valuable to court martial, President Davis promoted Forrest to major general and sent him off to Mississippi, far away from Bragg.

In Chattanooga, Rosecrans also had his troubles. With their major supply lines interrupted, the bluecoats went on short rations and thousands of draft animals died from hunger . What's more, in the aftermath of Chickamauga, the war department decided to send the hero of Vicksburg, U.S. Grant, to fix things in the Army of the Cumberland.

Grant, in fact, had just been promoted to department commander and, in short order, would give George Thomas the position which Rosecrans held. Arriving in Chattanooga on October 23, he found the situation serious indeed and proceeded with a plan to lift Confederate control of the supply routes.

On October 27, "Fighting Joe" Hooker--who had been so thoroughly demoralized by Lee at Chancellorsville-- led reinforcements toward Chattanooga from a Union supply base in Bridgeport, Alabama. Hooker's men linked up with the besieged garrison at Brown's Ferry, and the Tennessee River opened to Union supply boats. This so-called "cracker line" brought much-needed rations and equipment into the city. In one of the war's few night battles, Confederates tried and failed to recapture the bridgehead.

Despite this aggressive show of Union strength, in early November, Bragg ordered Longstreet to head north on a futile assignment to retake Knoxville. That city had been captured by Major General Ambrose Burnside, another eastern commander ordered into western exile after being defeated by Lee.

Sending off Longstreet rid Bragg of another hostile subordinate, but it also took troops he would soon need. Longstreet's campaign failed following a bloody assault on Knoxville's fortifications. After wintering in the wilderness of east Tennessee, he wound his way back home to the Army of Northern Virginia just in time for the start-up of 1864's spring-time slaughter.

Meanwhile, at Chattanooga, more Union reinforcements arrived: Major General William Sherman with 17,000 men.

On November 23, Grant took the offensive. His troops captured Rebel forward positions on Orchard Knob in front of Missionary Ridge. The next day, Hooker's men attacked Bragg's left and forced the Rebels off the towering summit of Lookout Mountain. This "battle above the clouds" opened the way for the Union army to threaten Bragg's retreat route into Georgia. The military situation was quickly changing.

Grant won his victory on November 25, when an all-day struggle against the Confederates on Missionary Ridge ended with the late-afternoon rout of Bragg's army. Union troops sent to take Confederate entrenchments along the base of the ridge continued forward--without orders--and determinedly scaled the heights. As Grant and his subordinates watched in astonishment, the extemporaneous advance sent the Rebels running. Bragg himself narrowly escaped capture. Only a stout rearguard action by the troops of Irish-born Major General Patrick Cleburne prevented the ruin of Army of the Tennessee. The Union defeat at Chickamauga had been avenged.

The Rebels retreated fifty miles to Dalton, Georgia, before halting and going into winter quarters. On November 28, Braxton Bragg submitted his resignation as commander of the Army of the Tennessee. With the North controlling the gateway to Georgia, Jefferson Davis would have to find a new general to keep the Yankees out of the state.

The Hanging of Sam Davis

On November 19, 1863, Private Sam Davis, formerly of the First Tennessee Infantry and now one of General Bragg's scouts, found himself captured by Union cavalry. Like many clothes-poor Confederates, Davis wore a Federal overcoat which had been dyed brown on top of his grey military jacket. His captors searched him and found maps and descriptions of Federal troops and fortifications in middle Tennessee. Suddenly, the 21-year-old prisoner took on more importance, and he was hustled before Brigadier General Grenville Dodge in Pulaski.

Dodge gave Sam Davis a grim choice: reveal his sources of information or be hung by the neck until dead. Davis refused to cooperate. One week after his capture, a court martial sentenced him to die the following day.

Davis accepted his fate stoically, and his captors admired his courage as they reluctantly performed their sad duty. While the executioner placed a rope around Davis' neck, a courier from General Dodge arrived to offer one last chance for life. Davis refused.

"If I had a thousand lives, I would lose them all here before I would betray my friends or lose the confidence of my informer. Thank General Dodge, but I cannot accept his terms."

Davis turned to the hangman and said his last words, "I am ready." The trap was sprung and, a few long moments later, he was dead.

To the South, Sam Davis became a martyr on the order of Nathan Hale in the Revolutionary War. To this day, he remains an example of both youthful courage and the tragic toll of war.

Confederate prisoners in Camp Douglas, Chicago, Illinois. (U.S. Army Military History Institute)

Prisons:
North & South

When the conflict began, being captured was generally a gentlemanly affair. Many prisoners gained freedom simply by signing a parole that they would not take up arms again until properly exchanged. Others waited in makeshift jails, such as the former tobacco warehouse which became Richmond's Libby Prison. In Washington, Rebels resided in the Old Capitol Prison, so named because it had served as the temporary Congressional meeting place after the British burned the real capitol during the War of 1812.

Regardless, most captives in the first year or two of war soon found themselves back home after being swapped for one of the enemy.

But as the war continued, the number of prisoners and prisons increased, and conditions gradually deteriorated. When U.S. Grant became general-in-chief of all United States forces, he ordered an end to the exchange of prisoners, recognizing that the trades provided far more benefit to the manpower-poor Confederacy than they did to the North.

As a result, both sides found themselves with a dramatic increase of captured enemy soldiers who had to be incarcerated and fed. In February 1864, the South sent the first captured Yankees to Andersonville, a wooden stockade in southwest Georgia which became the most infamous prison pen of the war.

Andersonville existed as a prison for only fifteen months, and it was fully operational for less than half that time. Conservative estimates indicate that some 13,000 Northern soldiers died from sickness and starvation within its walls. After the war, the Federals captured the camp commandant, Swiss-born Henry Wirz, and took him to Washington, where he was tried and hung for the horrors the prison produced.

Yet thousands of Southern soldiers also died when they were captives of the North. What's worse is that many of these soldiers succumbed while being held in a land of abundance, where--unlike the South--food and medical supplies were readily available. Ill-clothed Confederates accustomed to the warm weather of Dixie also suffered severely in the cold winter climes of camps like Elmira, New York, and Johnson's Island, Ohio.

In short, the record of the wartime prisons offers ample evidence on both sides of man's inhumanity to man.

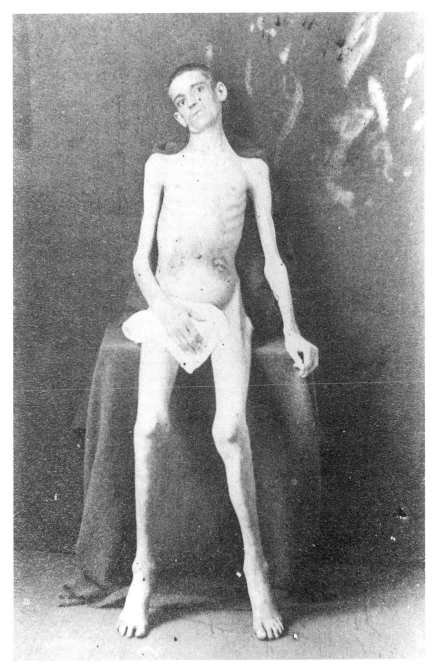

William B. Smith, 8th Kentucky Cavalry, in a photo taken at the U.S. General Hospital, Annapolis, Maryland, following his release from a Confederate prison in the spring of 1864. (U.S. Army Military History Institute)

1864

"We Were Turned Out of Our House by the Federal Officers..."

As the Northern armies occupied more and more of the Confederacy, relations with the Southern civilians were often strained. This letter, written by Felicia C. Chapman of Alabama, reflects the intense feelings of those difficult days.

Morgan Co. near Whitesburg
Feb. 16th 1864

Dr. John Erskine
Dear Sir:

Since your mother & other relatives are cut off from all communication with you, they requested as when we came out of the lines to write in their stead. Your mother's family as well as that of Mr. James Martin, and Dr. Wilkinson, were all well a few days ago. When we were turned out of our house by the federal officers, your mother kindly invited us to stay with her. We remained there nineteen days and we will never forget the kindness of every member of the family. Not withstanding the persecution of the Yankees, they are doing remarkably well, have plenty of provisions, and are in no way disturbed in their families, yet their plantations share the general stress of the county. Their house servants are all with them still except Henry, who ran away last summer. There is a Negro school at the Cumberland church and most of their younger servants attend it. Some officers called one day and demanded Mrs. Erskine's house for quarters, but Miss Sallie met them and talked, them out of it. The houses of a great many of your old friends are occupied by federal officers (illegible) others those of Messrs. Robert Watkins (who died a few weeks ago), Fackler, Beune, Mc Dowel, Gov. Clay, Withers Clay, Haus Yauner and many others. The families of Mr. Beune, Mr. Dowel and ours are the only ones that have been turned out entirely. Wellie is at home and has been having chills, but is now better. Mr. Jimmis is also at home.

Dr. Ross has not been disturbed yet in the church service, although he has the church crowded with Yanks every Sunday and gives it to them over the left shoulder, after his style. Several Yankee parties have been given in town, one at Jere Clemens, Maj. Fleming, Benj. Jolly, and others.

I suppose you have heard of the seven gentlemen that were sent out of the lines, and of Mrs. McDowel being sent to the penitentiary in Nashville, as a hostage for the traitor Sheets. I have written a long letter to Miss Meg Pickett, for Miss Lillie and we've all written many letters for our friends in Huntsville.

Mrs. Erskine gave me a memorandum of items to write to you, but amongst the many that she had from others it has been misplaced, and she deferred writing to you for several days with the hopes of finding it.

We are making our preparations to move South, and may perhaps settle in Tuscaloosa, or some other town convenient to our plantations in Sumter County.

Respectfully,
Felicia C. Chapman

Kilpatrick's Richmond Raid

As the armies rested in winter quarters at the beginning of 1864, Brigadier General Hugh Judson Kilpatrick hatched a plan to free the Union prisoners held in Richmond. On February 28, he took four thousand cavalrymen across the Rapidan River and rode all night toward the Confederate capital.

The next day, Kilpatrick split his force, sending five hundred men under Colonel Ulrich Dahlgren to circle around to the south of the city while Kilpatrick attacked from the north. Dahlgren, the 23-year-old son of Admiral John Dahlgren, had won honors and lost a leg during the Gettysburg Campaign. Refusing to remain out of action, he obtained an artificial limb and rejoined the army just in time for the raid.

On March 1, Kilpatrick reached the lightly manned defenses five miles outside of Richmond. There he hesitated and skirmished with the enemy militia while waiting for word of Dahlgren. None came.

That night pursuing Confederate cavalry under Major General Wade Hampton attacked the blue raiders. The Federals resisted Hampton's men but then headed southeast toward tidewater Virginia and the safety of the nearest Union lines. Eventually Kilpatrick's horsemen returned to the Army of the Potomac by boat.

Young Dahlgren did not return. Bedeviled by bushwackers, bad directions and flooded streams, he blundered into a Confederate ambush. Dahlgren boldly ordered the Rebels to surrender, and they responded with the volley that killed him.

On Dahlgren's body, the Confederates found documents indicating the Yankees planned to burn Richmond and kill Jeff Davis and his cabinet. This created a horrified furor in the South, though the North denied the authenticity of the papers.

The Confederates buried Dahlgren in an unmarked grave. Richmond Unionists learned the location and snatched the body, returning it to his family after the war. Dahlgren's artificial leg, after being temporarily displayed in a Richmond storefront, was fitted to one of John Mosby's Rebel rangers.

Grant Goes into the Wilderness

In March 1864, Abraham Lincoln promoted U.S. Grant to the rank of Lieutenant General and the position of General-in-Chief of the Armies of the United States. Though no one knew it at the time, this action marked the beginning of the end of the American Civil War.

Many observers in both blue and grey were skeptical of Grant's chances for success. True, he'd won victories out west, but he had never had to face Robert E. Lee and the Army of Northern Virginia either.

Such talk irritated Grant. He felt the eastern army spent too much time worrying what Lee might do to them, instead of concentrating on what they could do to Lee. Grant planned to change that. While George Meade, the victor of Gettysburg, remained in nominal command of the Army of the Potomac, Grant decided that he would travel with that army and directly oversee its operations.

Grant also intended to fully utilize the North's superior military might by coordinating the advance of all Union forces. At Chattanooga, Grant put his old friend, William Tecumseh Sherman, in command of the western army with orders to advance against Atlanta at the same time Grant commenced his campaign against Richmond. Grant also instructed Major General Benjamin Butler to bring troops from Fort Monroe up the Virginia peninsula and threaten Richmond. Yet another blue army, under Major General Franz Sigel, would move into the Shenandoah Valley, whose farms supplied much foodstuff for Lee's men.

The Army of the Potomac got underway on May 4, crossing the Rapidan River to the east of the Confederate's well-fortified winter camps. Grant hoped to turn Lee's flank, get between the Rebels and Richmond, and force a battle in open country. There the Northern numerical advantage of nearly two-to-one could be exploited to its fullest.

To do that, Grant first had to get his men through the dense wilderness south of the river, the same rough territory where Joe Hooker had come to woe just a year earlier.

Lee purposely did not contest the enemy's river crossing. He preferred to wait and strike Grant in the thickets of the Wilderness, where the Union superiority in men and artillery would be minimized.

The Confederates advanced eastward on two parallel roads, Lieutenant General Richard Ewell with the Second Corps on the Orange Turnpike and, to the south, Lieutenant General A.P. Hill, with the Third Corps on the Orange Plank Road. James Longstreet, rejoining the army after the failed campaigns in east Tennessee, would not arrive with the First Corps in time for the opening day's fighting.

On the early afternoon of May 5, the Battle of the Wilderness began. Warren's Fifth Corps attacked Ewell's greybacks who were deployed on both sides of the Orange Turnpike. The Yankees pushed the Rebels back, but their advanced slowed when reinforcements failed to arrive. Ewell counterattacked and recaptured the lost ground. The Rebels then entrenched.

To the south, A.P. Hill encountered the enemy guarding an intersection where the Orange Plank Road met the Brock Road, a key route for the Federal's southeastern movement. Hill attacked and enjoyed some success until Winfield Scott Hancock's Second Corps arrived to stabilize the blue line. A see-saw battle through the thickets and thorns continued until dark. During the melee, some of the heavy undergrowth caught fire, adding an even more menacing dimension to the inferno of fighting.

Lee had hoped to avoid a general engagement until Longstreet arrived. He expected the First Corps by the following morning but, when the dawn broke, they were not present. However, twenty thousand of Hancock's Union soldiers did descend on upon the Confederate right, smashing A.P. Hill's line and driving the defenders in disorder. As the blue wave whipped forward, only a thin line of artillery stood to stem the tide and determine the fate of Lee's army.

Then, as if on cue, Longstreet's Corps appeared. Robert E. Lee rode to meet them and found the hard-fighting Texas Brigade marching forward.

"Hurrah for Texas!" the usually reserved Lee shouted, waving his hat in the air. "Texans always move them!"

The great grey general turned and rode in front of the ragged ranks as if to lead them personally into battle. The Texans began to shout, "Lee to the rear!" and several men raced forward to turn the general's horse around. Longstreet himself arrived and promised to regain the lost ground if Lee agreed to take cover.

Longstreet kept his promise, and, by mid-day, he was organizing another assault to drive the Yankees even farther back. Then fate intervened. In an episode similar to "Stonewall" Jackson's wounding on nearly the same ground the year before, soldiers from a Virginia brigade mistook Longstreet and his staff for the enemy. They fired. Longstreet fell seriously wounded in the throat and shoulder, injuries which would bother him for the rest of his days. Another Confederate general, 28-year-old Micah Jenkins, was killed. Earlier, Jenkins had correctly boasted that he would never die from a Yankee bullet.

On May 6, Company I of the 57th Massachusetts numbered 86 men. After fighting at the Wilderness and Spotsylvania, it was reduced to nine members and commanded by a sergeant. (U.S. Army Military History Institute)

Fighting continued throughout the day. Near dusk, a Confederate attack on the Federal right flank stampeded the Union Sixth Corps, but darkness prevented the Southerners from exploiting their advantage.

In all, nearly 30,000 Americans became casualties during two days of some of the war's most savage slaughter. At the end, the situation stood much the same as when the battle began.

Dead confederate infantryman on the battlefield at Spotsylvania. (U.S. Army Military History Institute)

Spotsylvania: The Bloody Angle

In a similar situation the year before, "Fighting Joe" Hooker had accepted defeat and brought his men back to safety across the river. U.S. Grant was not "Fighting Joe." Puffing on his ever-present cigar, Grant examined his maps and ordered a continuation of the army's move to the southeast around Lee's flank. When the Union foot soldiers saw Grant and his staff riding south on the Brock Road, they knew what it meant and they cheered.

The crossroads of Spotsylvania Courthouse now became crucial to the plans of both armies. If Grant got there first, he would be on the best roads for a race to Richmond. If Lee controlled the crossroads, he could block the blue invaders once again.

It was a near thing, decided not by hours but by minutes. Horsemen from both sides reached the vicinity at the same time, but the arrival of Confederate infantry decided the matter.

To consolidate their claim on this precious piece of property, the Confederates began building earthworks, something soldiers had scorned at the beginning of the war but now did routinely. The engineers laid out a strong defensive position which followed a ridge line and was screened by vegetation.

One glaring weakness existed; in order to occupy the best ground, the V-shaped Confederate line had a conspicuous bulge near its center. The salient--called the "Mule Shoe" by the soldiers-- sat vulnerable to attack on three sides.

After maneuvering against the Confederate left flank on May 9, Grant decided to assault the "Mule Shoe" the following day. Twelve picked division, ordered not to fire until inside the Rebel works, made the attack in a formation which had more depth than width. They hoped to punch a hole in the "Mule Shoe" and then flank left and right, leaving support troops to continue ahead to stop any counterattack.

After some brief but fierce hand-to-hand fighting, the late-day assault succeeded in breaching the grey line. But expected reinforcements failed to arrive and the blue soldiers were forced to retreat.

Still, the method of attack showed promised and Grant decided to repeat the performance with more men early the following morning.

Philip Sheridan and his officers. Sheridan is standing on the steps in the middle of the front row. (U.S. Army Military Institute)

Now came one of those accidents of war. Lee believed an inaccurate report that Grant was on the march again. During the night, he ordered twenty-two cannons withdrawn from the "Mule Shoe" in preparation for pursuit. Then the massed Federal columns hit the salient, and the Confederates rushed through the rain to get their artillery back into position. Twenty of the guns were captured even before they could fire a shot.

During this fighting, part of the "Mule Shoe" earned another name: "The Bloody Angle."

In a war full of terrible combat, this was some of the worst. Men grappled hand-to-hand with clubbed muskets and bayonets. Firing was so heavy that an oak tree, nearly two feet in diameter, was cut down. If the Northerners succeeded, Lee's army would be sliced into two pieces and the war would be all but over.

As in the Wilderness, Lee tried to personally lead reinforcements into battle and, once again, his men ordered him to the rear. Though they could not expel the Unionists from the captured works, the Confederate counterattack bought time for a new line of defense to be built across the rear of the salient. After a full day of hellish struggle, the Confederates withdrew to the newly prepared position.

For nearly a week, comparative quiet prevailed as the two armies strengthened their already strong fortifications. On May 18, the Federals made one more try at cracking the Confederate line, but massed artillery blew them back. The next day, a Southern attack on the Union right quickly fizzled.

Approximately 17,500 Federals had been killed, wounded or captured at Spotsylvania. Confederate losses are unknown, but they had to be equally horrendous, probably 10,000 or greater. Following the carnage, once more, neither side had gained an advantage and Grant again gave orders for his troops to edge their way toward the southeast.

As the killing began at Spotsylvania, Grant sent his cavalry chief, Phil Sheridan, on a raid toward Richmond to draw off the enemy cavalry and disrupt Lee's communications. Sheridan boasted that he would whip J.E.B. Stuart and, in fact, he did more than that.

While fighting at Yellow Tavern, just outside the Confederate capital, the legendary Rebel general fell mortally wounded from a pistol ball fired by one of George Custer's Michigan troopers. After hearing the news, Lee said, "I can scarcely think of him without weeping."

"JEB" Stuart's last engagement: Federal and Confederate cavalry battle at Yellow Tavern, May 11, 1864 – by Edwin Forbes. (Sergeant Kirkland's Museum and Historical Society)

Cold Harbor:
The Battle Grant Would Always Regret

The Army of the Potomac's sideways advance slowly moved them closer and closer to Richmond. Lacking the manpower for an all-out offensive, Robert E. Lee knew that his opportunities for strategic maneuver were becoming more and more limited. As Lee himself acknowledged, if Grant reached the outskirts of Richmond, it would become a siege and then it would be but a mere matter of time.

Already, Ben Butler's Union troops from Fortress Monroe were on the south-side of the James River, just a few miles from Jeff Davis' executive mansion. Only a makeshift force of defenders had stopped them from entering the city.

The North Anna River, some two dozen miles above the Confederate capital, gave Lee another opportunity to entrench in a strong defensive position. It also gave him one of the last chances he ever would have to decisively defeat Grant.

On May 23, part of the Union army moved south of the North Anna where it held its ground against a Confederate attack. The next day, some distance to the east, Yankees under Winfield Scott Hancock occupied abandoned Confederate trenches also on the south side of the river.

Grant had made a mistake and Lee realized it. The Northern army was cut into thirds by the barrier of a waterway; its left flank and right flank were both below the river while the center remained above it. For Grant's right to reinforce his left would require two stream crossings.

Lee planned to crush Hancock before he could be reinforced, but fate intervened. Lee became so ill that he could not leave his tent, and death, wounds and illness had left no experienced officer to whom he could entrust the attack. During that last year of war, more than a third of the army's generals fell in battle. Grant soon recognized the blunder and pulled his army back to make yet another southeasterly move around Lee.

The armies next met at Cold Harbor, only a few miles from Richmond and close to the Seven Days battlefields where Lee had first taken command two long years before. Grant had tired of his flanking maneuvers and decided to punch his way through to the Confederate capital. On June 3, at 4:30 a.m., he launched the assault that he would always regret.

Advancing in double lines along a six-mile front, the Army of the Potomac charged the well-placed entrenchments of the Army of Northern Virginia. After three years of war, the Yankee veterans recognized a strong position when they saw it, and, before the charge, they pinned paper name tags to their coats so they could be identified if they fell. Many of them did fall. During the day, the bluecoats suffered almost 7000 casualties and were driven back to their own lines. The greycoats lost less than 1500.

The huge casualties from the Wilderness to Cold Harbor appalled the North, and Grant's detractors called him a "butcher." But Grant, who supposedly got a queasy stomach if served an undercooked cut of meat, knew that the Union could sustain the losses while the Confederacy could not. He continued on.

However, Cold Harbor made him realize that he could not batter his way into Richmond. Once again, he moved to the southeast and, in the process, deceived Robert E. Lee more completely than he was ever deceived at any time in the war.

Grant managed to steal a march and move his army across the James River, while the Confederate commander continued to believe the Yankees remained in place. With Lee unaware, Union troops moved toward Petersburg, twenty-three miles due south of Richmond. Capture of that city would break most of Richmond's rail connections and force the evacuation of the Confederate capital.

Petersburg was there for the taking, defended only by a small force of veterans and home guard, but the Federals failed to grasp the prize which was so easily within their reach. This gave Lee time to realize what had happened and rush troops to the scene.

The Federal failure to take Petersburg in early June was to prove quite costly in terms of American lives. Nine more months of bloody fighting and thousands of casualties would follow as both armies endured the strain of siege warfare.

Sherman Captures Atlanta

Jefferson Davis did not want to give Joe Johnston command of the Army of the Tennessee, but he had little choice. Since the early days of the war, relations between the two men had grown increasingly antagonistic, and Davis remembered all too well Johnston's cautious performance as McClellan made his way toward Richmond in 1862. Davis also no doubt felt that Johnston shared in the blame for the loss of Vicksburg. But the only other available officer with sufficient rank and stamina for a field command was P.G.T. Beauregard, and Davis liked the New Orleans Creole even less than he did Johnston. What's more, naming Johnston would help placate a vocal clique of anti-administration politicians with whom the general associated. Davis reluctantly made the appointment in December 1863.

The Army of the Tennessee approved of their new leader, and Johnston began work by reorganizing and refitting his command. New uniforms and better food went to the rank-and-file, and, throughout the winter, a rotating system of furloughs allowed the soldiers to visit their homes and families. Morale soared and, by the spring, the Army of the Tennessee stood ready to retake the field.

Of course, the old problem of manpower remained the same. In the spring of 1864, Johnston had perhaps 60,000 men. His opponent, William Tecumseh Sherman, had 100,000. These numbers gave Sherman the advantage he needed to sidestep Johnston's well-prepared positions in the rugged north Georgia countryside. That, in a nutshell, is the story of the Atlanta campaign.

The fighting began in early May when Sherman hit the Rebel line on Rocky Face Ridge near Dalton. These attacks were but a mask for a wide flanking movement that was winding its way around Johnston's left. Johnston soon had no choice but to make a night march in retreat to Resaca.

There Johnston again found a formidable defensive position with both his left and right securely anchored on rivers. Sherman attacked and failed. Johnston launched his own attack on Sherman's left, but any promise of success disappeared when word arrived that the army had again been flanked. Johnston ordered a retreat; he did not have enough men to hold the line at Resaca and still dispatch sufficient soldiers to whip the Yankees threatening his rear.

At Calhoun, the Confederates dug in again. This time, the Yanks threatened both flanks. The Rebels retreated once more.

Desperately seeking a way to seize the initiative, Johnston found it near Cassville on May 19 when he anticipated Sherman would take roads which would divide the blue army by as much as five miles. Johnston planned an ambush, but his usually aggressive subordinate, John B. Hood, balked and the plan failed.

The army retreated to a new position. Two of Johnston's three corps commanders protested the line was untenable, and Johnston bowed to their beliefs. Again, they retreated.

And so it went; Sherman by-passing any strong Southern positions and the Confederates missing those few opportunities to strike a blow when Sherman's superior numbers were separated. Battles were fought, but the outcome of the campaign was being determined by the Union army's ability to hold the enemy in place while it marched around their prepared defenses.

Finally, just above Atlanta, Sherman grew weary of his side-step strategy--even though it was working--and decided to try to break through a strong Rebel position on Kennesaw Mountain. The Yankees were repulsed with heavy losses. Sherman returned to his flanking maneuvers.

Johnston fell back to a mighty stronghold which his engineers had prepared to cover the major crossings along the Chattahoochee River, the last natural line of defense before the actual fortifications around Atlanta. In theory, the position was impregnable, but a dozen miles upstream part of the blue army found a vulnerable river crossing and immediately built their own unassailable earthworks. Johnston ordered another retreat.

The farther Sherman advanced, the more exposed and dependent he became upon the railroad out of Chattanooga. Throughout the campaign, the Confederates recognized the opportunity this presented, but they were unable to fully capitalize upon it.

Sherman, himself, feared that the cavalry of Nathan Bedford Forrest would wreck his communications. Instead, Forrest went after a strong column of Union raiders moving into Mississippi. Though he won his greatest victory at Brices Crossroads, historians still wonder if the Confederacy might have enjoyed a greater benefit had Forrest gone to Georgia.

Jefferson Davis had watched with increasing dismay as the Confederates gave ground toward Atlanta. With Sherman's crossing of the Chattahoochee, Davis' worst fears appeared to be coming true; he believed Johnston would evacuate the prized city without even putting up a fight. On July 17, Johnston received a telegram relieving him from command.

George Henry Thomas, the "Rock of Chickamauga." (U.S. Army Military History Institute)

In Johnston's place, Davis put Lieutenant General John B. Hood, a 33-year-old Kentuckian who won fame as a division commander in the Army of Northern Virginia. His left arm had been mangled on the second day at Gettysburg, and he had lost a leg leading his men at Chickamauga less than three months later. That winter, during his recovery in Richmond, Hood enjoyed entree to the capital's best social circles and won the confidence of the Confederate president.

Appointed to corps command in the Army of the Tennessee, he corresponded directly with Jeff Davis, and his letters played upon Davis' suspicions of Johnston's generalship. Before appointing Hood, Davis asked the advice of Hood's former commander, Robert E. Lee. Lee responded with praise for Hood's fighting prowess leading a division, but he discretely declined comment on Hood's ability to lead an entire army. Nevertheless, Hood got the command along with a temporary rank of full general.

As Yankee shells sailed into the city limits of Atlanta, Hood planned a bold offensive against his opponent. Only three days after his appointment, he struck the enemy north of town along Peachtree Creek. "The Rock of Chickamauga," George Thomas, commanded that part of the Union line, and he sent the Rebels reeling into Atlanta with nearly 5000 casualties.

Nevertheless, Hood quickly regrouped and tried hitting the invaders east of the city in what became known as the Battle of Atlanta. Despite a promising start and fierce fighting, this attack, too, ended in failure for the Confederates. Among the dead was Union Major General James McPherson, a 35-year-old West Pointer and a favorite of both Grant and Sherman. Sadly, McPherson had delayed taking a furlough to get married until the campaign ended.

A week later, the Confederates suffered another defeat at Ezra Church, and the military situation settled into a siege.

Sherman sent his cavalry to work against the railroads which supplied the city with provisions. Hood responded by sending his horsemen north to strike Sherman's rail connections. Neither effort produced the desired results, and, at the end of August, Sherman began moving his army to cut the Macon-and-Western line at Jonesboro. Hood thought the move was merely a diversion, and, after heavy fighting, the Unionists captured the railroad.

His rail connection cut, Hood had no choice but to abandon Atlanta. On the evening of September 1, distant explosions surprised the blue soldiers. They thought perhaps, another battle had begun. Instead, Hood had put the torch to his ammunition trains, serving notice that he was retreating. Sherman marched into the city the next day.

William Tecumseh Sherman. (U.S. Army Military History Institute)

The glad tidings reached the North right after that of another victory; on August 5, Rear Admiral David Farragut had seized control of Mobile Bay in Alabama, closing off yet another Confederate port.

"I Am Wiling to Come Home and See No Mor of the War..."

As Sherman's men threatened Georgia, Governor Joe Brown called up the state guards to help drive back the invaders. One of these was 30-year-old private M.L. House of the Georgia Cavalry. Here he writes to his wife of the fighting north of Atlanta.

July 1st 1864 Friday

Dear Elizabeth

As I rote in a hury the other day I will drop you a few lines to day this leaves me well hoping those line may find you enjoying the same blesing Brother & Z B Dallis is well the helth of the redgment is very good tho not anctious for a fite we ar three miles of the enemy lines and too miles in the rer of our lines held as a reserve the pickets keep up a con tin al fier we can her the canonading all a long the line Saturday morning July th 2 while I was riting yesterday we was caled in line and marched about too miles to the front we marched up the shells fell thick a round us but fortutionally nun of us was hurt about that time I herd our men rase a yell and I herd sence tha fetched too bateres about that time we was marched too miles back to wards the river to prevent a flank move ment we stretched out in a line to picket the enemy we re mane her in line this morning Thare is a brisk fire on our right this morning we is all right this morning I think tha shore will come off to day or to morrow I hav not got a leter from you since Brother came....(back to hom).....(my Address) M.L. House Co A 1st R edg. Car of Conl Pottle atlanta ga I have riten a bout three leters a weak since I hav bin out I do not now hwether you got them or not

My dear I never hav enjoyed beter helth in my life than I hav since I hav bin her I think I will get back to my good old home if the yankies donot get me I hav seen a pontoon brig crost the river on it and have seen the shells bust and herd a charge made and stood picket I have see a nuf to tell my children when I get old I am wiling to come home and see no mor of the war and I do hope it will not be long befor we can all come home and be at Peace Tell Doctor Quim to rite to me and Jeter Z Duch and rite all of the nuse good by for this time.

M.L. House
To Eliza House

The C.S.S. Alabama:
Rebel Raider or Pirate Ship?

Throughout the war, the Confederate Navy was a make-shift affair, generally relying upon captured vessels, converted civilian ships and whatever could be obtained abroad. In the last category fell the *C.S.S. Alabama*, built in England and whisked off to sea under the noses of protesting U.S. diplomats.

Captain Raphael Semmes, a native of Maryland and an old salt from the pre-war navy, led the *Alabama* on a spectacular two-year career during which it journeyed some 75,000 miles and captured sixty-four Northern merchant ships. The ill-disciplined crew consisted of an international mix of sailors. Few had any ties to the South but were enticed to serve with promises of plunder. Without ever entering a Confederate port, they sailed to Singapore and back, striking terror in any vessel flying the United States flag.

The success of the *Alabama* created an uproar in the North, and the blue navy searched the globe to bring this "pirate" to bay. In June, 1864, the *U.S.S. Kearsarge* found the raider, refitting in port at Cherbourg, France. Challenged to come out and fight, Semmes accepted on Sunday, June 19. After a one-hour battle, the *C.S.S. Alabama* went to a watery grave.

Semmes escaped to a nearby English ship and, eventually, made his way back to the Confederacy, where he was promoted to rear admiral and given charge of the James River Squadron.

Following the war, the Federal government arrested Semmes on charges of treason and piracy, but the case was finally dropped. The United States did, however, pursue claims against England for damages caused by the *Alabama* and other British-built Rebel raiders. In 1872, an international tribunal awarded the U.S. $15.5 million in gold.

One final note: another Confederate ship, the *C.S.S. Shenandoah*, was constructed in Scotland in 1864. It captured thirty-eight enemy merchant vessels, most of them after the war had already ended. In August, 1865, while in the Arctic Ocean, the crew finally became convinced that the South actually had lost. They set sail for Liverpool, turning their orphan ship over to British authorities in November 1865.

A black sailor aboard the *USS Vermont*. (U.S. Army Military History Institute.)

The North was outraged by reports of black Union soldiers being slaughtered at Fort Pillow, Tennessee on April 12, 1864. (Frank Leslie's Illustrated Newspaper, May 7, 1864)

Black Soldiers and the Fight for Freedom

As soon as the war began, escaped slaves found their way to Union lines in search of freedom. Generally without resources, many hung around the army camps where they went to work as teamsters and laborers.

Not until the middle of the war did the Federal government accept the enlistment of blacks as actual soldiers. Then they were generally used as garrison troops or to perform duties the white soldiers wished to avoid. The black regiments were paid less than white troops and were governed by white officers. There were other slights, too. For example, the 30th United States Colored Troops were issued second-hand muskets, which some members later exchanged for the brand-new guns of a sleeping white regiment.

The question was: would they fight? They proved they would at Fort Wagner in Charleston Harbor, at the Crater in Petersburg, at Nashville, and at nearly 450 other engagements. Some 37,000 became casualties.

The ex-slaves feared capture. When Nathan Bedford Forrest's men stormed Fort Pillow, Tennessee, in 1864, only fifty-eight of the 262 black soldiers were taken prisoner. The North charged it was a massacre, reporting that Forrest's men had yelled, "No quarter! Kill the damn niggers!" The South claimed it was not a massacre, that the black troops had simply fought tenaciously.

There were, of course, many blacks with the Confederate Army, and no doubt some of these men actually shouldered a musket in battle. Nevertheless, the overwhelming majority served as servants, teamsters, and manual laborers.

As the South's manpower shortage grew, so did the debate over enlisting persons of color. This struck at the very heart of the institution of slavery and was resisted until the very end. Southern statesman and general Howell Cobb declared, "If slaves will make good soldiers, our whole theory of slavery is wrong."

However, in the waning weeks of the war, after the proposal received the endorsement of Robert E. Lee, enlisting black men was authorized by the Confederate government. Only a few ever made it into uniform and none ever saw action.

Conversely, by 1865, 200,000 Union soldiers and sailors were persons of color, equal to about ten percent of all Northern troops.

A Northern officer with his pipe and his servant. (U.S. Army Military History Institute)

The Burning of Chambersburg

Chambersburg, Pennsylvania, was a three-time loser in the War Between the States. Located just above the Mason-Dixon line, it was on the main invasion route coming out of Virginia's Shenandoah Valley. The first Rebels reached the town in October 1862, when J.E.B. Stuart's cavalry made a raid around McClellan's army after the Battle of Antietam. The Southerners stayed only a few hours, destroyed some military supplies, and then rode away to escape their pursuers.

The following year, Lee's Army of Northern Virginia passed through town during the Gettysburg Campaign. Once again, the Confederates behaved themselves about as well as any invading army could be expected to have behaved.

It was a different story in July 1864. By then Union Major General David Hunter had become notorious for burning houses and destroying property in the Shenandoah Valley. The Confederates wanted revenge, and Jubal Early sent cavalry under Brigadier General John McCausland to get it. Reaching Chambersburg, the grey riders demanded $100,000 in gold or $500,000 in greenbacks as compensation for the destruction in Virginia.

The townspeople could not pay. McCausland ordered the 3000 residents to evacuate their homes, and then the Confederates set fire to the town, turning two-thirds of it to ashes.

Heading south, McCausland repeated his ransom demands in Hancock, Maryland, but the timely arrival of Union cavalry saved the town. Later, at Moorefield, West Virginia, Federal soldiers again caught up with McCausland and soundly whipped the raiders.

The burning of Chambersburg stands out because it was the only town north of the Mason-Dixon line to suffer such a fate. In the battle-torn South, wanton destruction had become commonplace as the fighting entered its end game. The war had long since ceased being glamorous.

Early and Sheridan in the Shenandoah

Often called the "Granary of the Confederacy," Virginia's Shenandoah Valley became an important source of foodstuff for Lee's army throughout the war. In the spring of 1864, Grant sent troops under Major General Franz Sigel to cut off supplies from the region.

The Confederates were hard pressed to resist. Major General John Breckinridge, who later would become the Confederacy's last secretary of war, gathered a makeshift command and rushed to meet the invaders. With the valley's defenders marched about 250 young cadets called from their studies at the Virginia Military Institute in Lexington.

On May 15, the two armies met at the little town of New Market, and Sigel's force was defeated. Among the Confederate casualties were fifty-seven V.M.I. cadets either killed or wounded.

The victory bought time for the valley, but not much time. By June, blue troops under David Hunter went all the way to Lexington where they exacted revenge by burning the Virginia Military Institute. Hunter then turned east toward Lynchburg, threatening Lee's army from yet another direction.

Fully occupied in dealing with Grant, Lee dispatched his "bad old man," Jubal Early, to take troops which Lee could ill-afford to spare and save Lynchburg from capture.

Early got there just in time. To delay the Yankee attack, empty trains had been running in and out of the city to fool Hunter into believing the scant defenders had already been reinforced. When Early actually did arrive, he chased the Unionists deep into the hills of West Virginia. This left the Shenandoah Valley open to Early's Confederates, and "Old Jube" led his men northward. Taking a leaf from "Stonewall" Jackson's 1862 campaign, he planned to threaten Washington; in fact, he came very close to capturing it.

Early entered Maryland, whipped an outnumbered Union force on the Monocacy River, and then proceeded to the outskirts of the national capital.

On July 12, Abraham Lincoln watched as the blue and grey skirmished around the defenses of Washington. Then Early retreated. Troops from Grant's army, the battle-tested Sixth Corps, had arrived to reinforce Washington.

The Confederates went back to occupy the valley, but Grant determined that they should not hold the prize. Major General Phil Sheridan assembled an army at Harpers Ferry, and, on September 19, his 40,000 men routed Early's 11,500 at Winchester. That town had changed hands many times during the war, but now it would stay under Union control until the end.

Early reassembled his men in a strong defensive position along Fisher's Hill, just south of Strasburg. At least, it would have been a strong defensive position had he had enough men to adequately defend it all. As it was, the Yankees discovered that the Rebel left flank was weak and, on September 22, the veterans of Early's little army once again fled in disorder.

With these decisive victories, Sheridan controlled the Shenandoah, and he moved his troops as far south as Harrisonburg, systematically devastating the rich agricultural region just at its time of harvest. Then, believing the campaign had ended, he withdrew north toward Winchester.

On October 19, the Union army rested peacefully along the waters of Cedar Creek. No danger seemed imminent. The Southerners were not believed to be either nearby or in any condition to attack.

But, at five a.m. that morning, the greybacks stormed into the blue encampment, screaming their fierce Rebel yell and driving the Yankee pickets before them. Rudely awakened from their slumbers, many of the surprised Federals ran for their lives, and, by mid-morning, Jubal Early felt certain that he had secured a great victory.

Sheridan had other ideas. Returning from meetings in Washington, he had spent the previous night in Winchester, where he had heard the distant gunfire that morning. Mounting his horse, "Little Phil" galloped down the Valley Turnpike to see what had happened. En route, he met the retreating soldiers of his command and exhorted them in strong language to turn and retake their camps. Sheridan's men believed in him and many did go back to face the Rebels.

But even before Sheridan arrived, the tide had begun to turn. Hungry Confederates paused to plunder the rich spoils in the enemy tents, and the momentum of the surprise assault gradually spent itself. Many elements of the Union army had rallied and were ready to reenter the fray.

At four o'clock that afternoon, Sheridan launched a counter-assault. The impact sent Early's men scampering south on the Valley Turnpike. The Confederates lost not only all the artillery they had captured that morning, but also twenty-five cannons of their own.

Early was truly whipped. Public opinion would, eventually, force Lee to relieve him from command. As winter approached, the half-starved grey soldiers defending Petersburg knew that their rations would not be supplemented by the rich stores which the fertile farms of Shenandoah Valley had once provided.

"The Old Sixth Took Them in Hands and Whipt Them..."

Jacob Claar, a 26-year-old carpenter from Bedford, Pennsylvania, joined the 138th Pennsylvania Volunteers as a private in August, 1862. After spending the first part of the war guarding Maryland railroads, the regiment saw action with the Army of the Potomac and, in the fall of 1864, served with Sheridan in the Shenandoah Valley.

Camp Near Cedar Run
October 21st 1864

Dear Wife

I take my pen in hand to in form you that I am well at present I hope when these few lines Come to hand the(y) will find you in the Same State of health I received your kind and well Come letter this evening I was glad to hear from home and that you ware all well at that time I will in form you that we had a hard Battle on the 19th of this month the Rebels Drove the 8th and 19th Corps and the old Sixth took them in hands and whipt them and Drove them and took Sixty pises of Artilry ambulunc and wagons and prisners quite a number we lost one killed and two wounded in our Company we are garding the Captured truck at army head-qurters I don't know how long we will Stay here I have no particular news to write this time I think I must bring my letter to a Close for this time nothing more at present But Remember your Dear husband

Jacob C Claar

Custer:
The Boy General

Anyone looking at his academic record would never have guessed what the future held for West Point cadet George Armstrong Custer. A careless student whose worst subject his senior year was cavalry tactics, he came in at the very bottom of the second Class of 1861. Due to the war, this class--originally scheduled to graduate in 1862--had its studies abbreviated and, three days after leaving the academy, Custer found himself fighting Rebels at Bull Run.

Custer served on the staff of army commander George McClellan and, after McClellan's departure, he joined cavalry chief Alfred Pleasonton. Pleasonton liked the daring young captain and had him promoted to brigadier general at the tender age of twenty-three.

Custer quickly proved his worth. Just days after his promotion, he distinguished himself in combat against J.E.B. Stuart at Gettysburg. When Phil Sheridan took charge of the Army of Potomac's cavalry corps, Custer's aggressive style was a perfect fit, and he played a key role in the North's 1864 conquest of the Shenandoah Valley. Except for the time he stole away to be with his new bride, Libbie, he tirelessly waged a relentless war against the Confederates.

In that era, general officers had wide latitude in the type and style of uniform they wore; Custer took full advantage. One of his outfits was described as a black-velvet jacket with elaborate, gold lace trim and a double row of gold buttons. The wide collar of a navy shirt turned out over the jacket while a red bandana, top boots and a broad-brimmed, black hat added to the costume. With his long, blond hair flying in the wind, Custer, according to one observer, resembled a circus rider gone mad.

Some were put off by Custer's self-aggrandizing nature, but his charismatic leadership and his ability to whip the enemy made him a favorite among the rank-and-file. Soldiers under his command proudly boasted of "Custer's luck," although they also grumbled about the long hours in the saddle that "Iron Butt" made them endure.

At the end of the war, Custer was a genuine hero to the people of the North. Peace, however, meant a smaller army, and he reverted from being a major general of volunteers to the regular rank of lieutenant colonel. Sent to the west, he became a controversial Indian fighter and suffered through a court martial for being absent from his post without authorization.

In the Peninsular campaign of 1862, Custer distinguished himself as a brilliant cavalry officer. Brought to George McClellan's attention, he was promoted to captain of volunteers, only to be demoted to first lieutenant upon McClellan's retirement. (Library of Congress)

In June 1876, Custer and more than 250 men of the Seventh Cavalry were annihilated by Sioux warriors in the Battle of the Little Big Horn. The flamboyant soldier who enjoyed so much early success in the Civil War is today best remembered for his later role in one of the worst defeats in American military history.

George Armstrong Custer with his wife, Libbie. (U.S. Army Military History Institute)

Southern soldiers killed in the trenches of Fort Mahone during the final assault on Petersburg, Virginia. (U.S. Army Military History Institute)

The Trench War

In many ways, the siege of Petersburg was a precursor of the awful trench fighting of World War One. For nine months, the armies held their ground as Grant tried to find a way to capture the city that Lee desperately needed to hold.

In the ranks of the 48th Pennsylvania, a group of coal miners thought they had a way to break the stalemate. They would tunnel beneath the Rebel earthworks and blow a hole in their lines. Grant gave his skeptical approval and the project proceeded.

On the morning of July 30, four tons of gunpowder exploded under the Confederate trenches, tossing men and equipment into the air. Union troops charged into the crater that was created as the stunned Rebels tried to understand what had happened.

But once in the crater, the Yankees faltered and grew disorganized. The Confederates brought up reinforcements and the gambit became a disaster for the Union soldiers. In all, they suffered nearly 3800 casualties while Southern losses were, perhaps, 1500.

As the siege continued, Grant gradually worked his lines southwest, taking possession of the Weldon Railroad and straining Lee's limited ability to man the lengthy line of earthworks.

At City Point, Grant's headquarters, a huge supply base provided all the arms, equipment and foodstuffs that the Northerners needed. Lacking such abundance, Confederate cavalry under Wade Hampton slid behind Union lines to successfully rustle three thousand head of Yankee cattle. As the grey soldiers later dined on Northern beef, they amused themselves by making mooing sounds across the trenches at their enemy.

That summer, with the presidential election approaching, Abraham Lincoln feared that a war-weary North might turn him out of office. To run against Lincoln, the Democrats nominated none other than George B. McClellan, who had proven so timid as commander of the Army of the Potomac. Among the Democrats were many so-called "Copperheads" who opposed Lincoln's war policy and favored a negotiated peace settlement with the South.

But Sherman's capture of Atlanta and Sheridan's successes in the Shenandoah reassured voters that a final victory was within sight. Lincoln easily won re-election. Soldiers, voting in the field, gave "Old Abe" the lion's share of their ballots.

Sherman's March to the Sea

Following the fall of Atlanta, Jefferson Davis embarked upon a morale-building trip to the Army of the Tennessee. He met with the crippled young lion whom he had put in command of the army and listened as Hood outlined a plan to move north, forcing Sherman to follow. Like many of Hood's plans, it was both audacious and flawed. But Davis approved the general concept and, on his way home, the president made public speeches predicting that the Army of the Tennessee would soon be back on its home soil.

Sherman read the reprint of Davis' remarks in Southern newspapers, and he took Davis at his word. Here was the flaw in Hood's strategy. When Hood moved north, Sherman had already developed a different plan.

Sherman sent George Thomas to pull together a sufficient force of the North's scattered troops to deal with Hood while Sherman took off on a remarkable march to the sea. The idea was that Sherman would cut loose from his supply lines and lead his men on a hell-raising expedition right through the heart of Georgia. They would live off the land, taking what they needed and destroying the rest. At the end, much of the state's agricultural and industrial production would lay in ashes.

And that's just about how it turned out. Except for some cavalry and homeguard units which Sherman's veterans pushed easily aside, Hood's move north left Georgia more or less defenseless.

Having already ordered all civilians out of Atlanta, Sherman put the town to the torch on November 15 in order to prevent it from being of any further military use. Then, with his army split into two columns across a front that, at times, was 60 miles wide, he set off for Savannah, 275 miles away.

Sherman later became famous for saying "war is hell." That is something he certainly proved on his march. He declared that he would "make Georgia howl" and, indeed, he did. His name became anathema to the people of the South and, years later, an uproar arose when Sherman's son planned a visit to the Peach State.

The Yankee "bummers" plundered plantations, burned barns and killed livestock, even shooting dogs which they thought may have been used to track escaped slaves. Often the bluecoats helped themselves to jewelry and other valuables; such robbery went against orders, but only the most flagrant offenders received any punishment. The Yankees' plundering behavior prompted lurking Rebel horsemen to shoot on sigh any stray enemy soldiers unlucky enough to have been caught.

Industrial facilities were totally destroyed. Railroads were another target; the iron ties, heated and twisted into a useless shape, became known as "Sherman's hairpins."

In six weeks, the invaders grew greatly skilled in all manner of destruction, and the lonely, brick chimneys of burned mansions and barren farms marked the path they had traveled. The devastation was such that some soldiers wrote of starving women offering their bodies in exchange for food.

As the army moved through Georgia, a growing band of freed slaves followed. The number seemed to jump with each plantation they passed. Perhaps as many as 25,000 tagged along on the march, a tremendous encumbrance for a fighting force, but Sherman could find no way to restrain them.

Reaching Milledgeville, the bluecoats vandalized the Georgia state house and held a mock session of the legislature, during which they repealed the state's ordinance of secession. Sherman slept that night in the recently abandoned governor's mansion.

Southern predictions that the raid would end in a disaster like Napoleon's march on Moscow forgot that there is a scarcity of snow in the South. Only grey soldiers could save Georgia, and there weren't enough of them to do the job.

For the North, it was as if Sherman had crawled into a hole and disappeared, for all communication ceased after he left Atlanta. Then, on December 22, a telegram for President Lincoln traveled across the wires. It read, "I beg to present you as a Christmas gift the City of Savannah with 150 heavy guns & plenty of ammunition & also about 25,000 bales of cotton. W. T. Sherman, Major General."

Clearly the end was near. The year before, at Vicksburg, the Confederacy had been chopped in half. After Sherman's march to the sea, it was cut into thirds.

Slaughter at Franklin; Disaster at Nashville

As he led his men north away from Atlanta and the rampaging blue army, John B. Hood dreamed of glory. With a quick march, perhaps he could capture Nashville and take his army to the banks of the Ohio River. He might even turn east and help Lee defeat Grant. There was no end to the magnificent victories waiting to be won in the fertile imagination of the young commander.

But the general's body was crippled from wounds and the exertions of active field duty carried him to the limits of his endurance. He may have used opiates ease his pain, but they also would have cost him the clarity of mind a successful military leader needs.

Hood came close to a magnificent triumph. Moving north, the Rebels engaged in a foot race with Major General John Schofield's Yankees, who were desperately trying to get back to Nashville where Thomas was assembling his army.

At Spring Hill, Tennessee, Hood's troops moved into position to block the road the enemy needed. Then, in one of the greatest lost opportunities and strangest mysteries of the war, the Confederates failed to close the trap. They simply went into camp instead of cutting the Yankees' escape route. That night, Schofield scurried to safety, his retreating columns within an easy musket shot of the sleeping Rebels.

Whose fault this was has never been clearly established; in truth, the high command of the Army of the Tennessee had failed again, and there was enough blame to go around for everyone.

The next morning, November 30, Hood became enraged when he realized the Yankees were gone. Hoping to salvage the situation, he pursued Schofield eight miles to Franklin, where the bluecoats had taken a strong defensive position along the Harpeth River.

Surveying the scene from a distant hilltop, Hood ordered an attack. Several of his generals, impressed by the enemy's imposing earthworks, suggested a flanking moving instead. Hood refused, saying that he preferred to fight the Yankees in Franklin where they had only a few hours to entrench, rather than in Nashville where they had had several years to prepare.

Just before sunset that fateful autumn day, some 20,000 Confederates--thousands more than had participated in Pickett's Charge at Gettysburg--moved across an open field toward the enemy. Two Federal brigades had mistakenly stayed in front of the main Union breastworks, and the confusion of their return allowed the center of the Confederate line to storm the Yankee defenses. Savage fighting ensued as a Union reserve brigade counter-attacked and beat the Rebels back.

It was a costly failure for John Hood. Though Schofield took advantage of darkness to continue his retreat to Nashville, he left behind some 7,000 Confederate casualties, including six dead grey generals. Since Hood held the field, he issued a proclamation congratulating his troops upon their success, but it was a hollow boast. After this most terrible of days, the Army of the Tennessee would never be the same.

And so the campaign played out to what was, after the failure at Franklin, a preordained conclusion. Hood marched his bloodied and ragged soldiers to the outskirts of Nashville, where they were too weak to assail the strong fortifications.

Instead, they threw up works of their own and waited until George Thomas had everything in place to come out and inflict a crushing blow. Thomas did exactly that on December 15, driving the Rebel line back two miles. The next day, Thomas attacked again and, despite valiant resistance, sent most of Hood's army running in confusion.

Nathan Bedford Forrest's cavalry fought bitter skirmishes with the pursuing Yankee horsemen while what remained of Hood's once grand command escaped into Alabama. When he had taken charge of the army at Atlanta six months earlier, it had numbered 50,000 soldiers. After Nashville, even with the addition of Forrest's horsemen, it mustered perhaps 18,000.

On that sad march, pelted by ice and snow, someone came up with a bitter parody of "The Yellow Rose of Texas":

> And now I'm going Southward
> My heart is full of woe
> I'm going back to Georgia
> To find my Uncle Joe
> You may talk about your Beauregard
> And sing of General Lee
> But the gallant Hood of Texas
> Played hell in Tennessee

On January 13, 1865, John Hood resigned from the command of the Army of the Tennessee.

1865

Sherman Moves North

On January 31, 1865, with the end of the rebellion in sight, the United States House of Representatives approved the Thirteenth Amendment to the Constitution, outlawing the institution of slavery. Its passage was a near thing; the measure had only three votes more than the two-thirds majority required by law.

Regardless, with victory in sight, the national government finally had committed to itself that the reunited country would no longer be half-slave and half-free.

That same month, William Tecumseh Sherman began another effort to hasten the collapse of the Confederacy. After enjoying the Christmas holidays in Savannah and giving his troops a well-deserved rest, he set off into South Carolina to offer them a taste of what Georgia had already experienced.

If anything, it was even worse. "Uncle Billy's bummers" felt that, as the first state to leave the Union, South Carolina bore a special responsibility for causing the conflict. So there was hell to pay as the Yankees advanced through the palmettos that winter.

Sherman did not head for Charleston, but his entry into the state caused that symbolic city to be evacuated by its defenders. Instead, Sherman marched toward the capitol at Columbia.

As in Georgia, the Confederates had little to stop him. What troops there were stood stood scattered, attempting to protect too many different points. Cavalry general Wade Hampton brought horsemen from Lee's army to help defend his native state, but only succeeded in creating a controversy over who started the blaze when Columbia caught fire. Sherman said the Confederates lit cotton bales when they evacuated the city. Hampton claimed the burning was another example of Yankee vandalism. Both were probably correct.

When Sherman reached North Carolina, the Confederates tried one last time to stop him. Joe Johnston had returned to command the remaining troops, including some of those long-suffering souls who had survived John Hood's disasters at Franklin and Nashville.

Sherman's troops were moving across the state in two columns. At Bentonville, on March 19, Johnston struck, hoping to destroy one column before the other could come to its assistance. The fighting lasted until dark, but the Confederates failed to achieve the breakthrough they needed.

Union reinforcements arrived the next day and the Rebels withdrew to entrenchments. More fighting followed until Johnston called for a retreat. What was left of the ill-starred Army of the Tennessee had been in its final major battle.

Ruins of Richmond after its capture, reflected in the Canal Street Basin. (U.S. Army Military History Institute)

Richmond Falls and Lee Surrenders

Meanwhile, that winter in Richmond, Robert E. Lee was given overall command of the Confederate armies, a promotion which many realized came too late to accomplish any good. The situation was now all but hopeless.

Confederate Vice President Alexander Stephens and two others had been dispatched as peace commissioners to meet with Abraham Lincoln that February. Lincoln offered peace but only if the rebellious states returned to the Union. Those terms Jeff Davis would never accept.

Lee understood that the spring would mean a resumption of campaigning by the massive Federal force tightening a noose around Petersburg and Richmond. Looking at the thin ranks of his beloved Army of Northern Virginia, Lee also knew that he could not adequately man the increasingly long line of entrenchments required to hold back the blue tide. But Lee was game to the end and he tried to take the offensive one last time.

In the pre-dawn of March 25, the Confederates quietly cleared away the barricades in front of their lines, and almost half Lee's army moved through the mists to capture Fort Stedman only 150 yards away. Once it was in their possession, the Southerners hoped to separate the Northern army from its supply base at City Point and then, somehow, force the overwhelming enemy army to retreat.

The plan stood, at best, the slimmest chance of success. The Confederates captured the fort, but could not break out beyond its walls. By eight a.m., it was clear the assault had failed and Lee sent word for his men to return to their lines. Many ran the gauntlet of fire back to the Confederate earthworks, but others simply surrendered. As they marched to the rear, these prisoners were amazed to see a review of troops underway for President Lincoln. Their surprise attack, the heaviest punch Lee could throw, had not even come close to testing the limits of Union might.

Lee had tried and failed. Now came Grant's turn. He feared that, one morning, he would awake to find that Lee had stolen a march on him, abandoning the Petersburg trenches and heading to join Joseph Johnston in North Carolina. Grant moved to prevent that.

The Southside and Danville Railroads were Lee's last supply links to the outside world. Lee would need the Southside to move his troops to North Carolina. At the end of March, Grant sent Phil Sheridan, who had just returned from the Shenandoah Valley, to destroy these lines.

Battle-hardened soldiers of the 2nd Rhode Island Infantry. (U.S. Army Military History Institute)

Anticipating the move, Lee dispatched a force of cavalry and infantry under the command of George Pickett of Gettysburg fame. Outnumbered by more than two to one, the Confederates lost the Battle of Five Forks on April 1; Richmond and Petersburg could no longer be held.

On the early morning of April 2, Grant ordered an assault against the lightly manned Confederate lines around Petersburg. The defenders fought ferociously, buying time with their lives for Lee to organize a retreat. Among the casualties that day was Confederate Lieutenant General A.P. Hill, whose timely arrival had saved the army so long ago at Antietam.

That spring morning, Jefferson Davis attended services at St. Paul's Church in Richmond. An anxious courier arrived with a dispatch and Davis left his pew immediately. That evening, he and other members of the government took a train to Danville where they hoped to carry on the Confederate nation.

For Richmond, a hellish night lay ahead. The government warehouses, full of supplies the army could have used during the prior winter, were set ablaze to prevent their capture by the Yankees. The fires spread and soon engulfed a large section of the city. When the last grey soldiers left, drunken mobs looted shops and disorder reigned. At about 8:15 on the morning of April 3, Union troops entered the capital, restoring order and extinguishing the fires. As the "Stars-and-Stripes" rose above the Virginia statehouse, hunger forced many of the city's matrons to swallow their pride and ask the hated Yankees for rations. For Richmond, the war was over, but the enemy occupation had just begun.

Robert E. Lee's ordeal continued. He tried to hustle his disintegrating army to the southwest, hoping to bypass the Federals and still link up with Johnston. Then the combined Rebel armies might beat Sherman and, in turn, whip Grant. It was the tiniest fading ember of hope, but it was still enough for men to continue on killing and dying.

Reaching Amelia Courthouse, Lee expected a trainload of rations to be waiting for his tired troops. But the order had somehow miscarried, and the gaunt Confederates found only ammunition, harnesses and caissons. The fugitive army lost precious time as hungry men combed the red-clay countryside in search of anything edible.

During those hours, Grant's aggressive army continued its relentless pursuit. They knew the war was near its end and they wanted it to come quickly.

At Saylers Creek on April 6, the Yankees captured nearly a quarter of Lee's army: six generals and almost eight thousand men. Seeing the disaster, Lee let go of his customary reserve and exclaimed, "My God! Has the army dissolved?" Among those taken prisoner that Black Thursday was Lee's own son, George Washington Custis Lee.

What remained of the crumbling army continued its desperate flight westward, any move to the south and the Carolinas blocked by fast-traveling Union columns. After dark on April 7, a courier brought a message to Lee from Grant which urged the Rebel's surrender. Lee silently passed the paper to Lieutenant General James Longstreet, who handed it back and said, "Not yet."

Nevertheless, Lee replied with a note asking what terms would be offered, and a correspondence between the opposing generals continued through the next day. That evening, as the Confederates neared Appomattox Courthouse, they found a solid line of blue blocking their route. The next morning, Lee's men tried and failed to fight their way through. Their commander reluctantly concluded that there was no other alternative except to go and see General Grant. It was April 9, Palm Sunday.

They met in the home of Wilmer McLean, a refugee who had relocated to south-central Virginia after the fighting at Bull Run had swept across his property. Now the war would end in his parlor.

Lee arrived first, immaculately dressed in his best grey uniform with a bright sash and a magnificent dress sword. Only a single aide accompanied him.

Grant entered the room with a dozen officers. He wore mud-spattered boots, no sword and a private's coat which bore his insignia of rank. The two generals shook hands and made small talk about the old army. Grant knew Lee from when they both had served in the Mexican War. Lee remembered that they had met, but admitted he could not recollect any of Grant's features.

Then Lee drew their attention to the business at hand. Grant's terms were generous; the Confederates would be paroled and allowed to return home. Officers could keep their sidearms, and anyone claiming ownership of a horse or mule would be allowed to take it. Lee remarked that that would have a happy effect upon his men and asked if Grant could supply rations to his starving soldiers. Grant agreed, making available some Confederate supplies which he had recently captured.

After Lee departed, the Union artillery began banging away in boisterous celebration. Grant ordered it stopped, not wishing to exhault in the downfall of his foe.

Upon Lee's return to camp, expectant soldiers crowded about his horse and asked if it was true that they were surrendered. Lee struggled to hold his emotions in check.

"Men, we have fought this war together, and I have done the best I could for you. You will all be paroled and go to your homes until exchanged." Then, as tears welled in his eyes, he realized he could not say more and simply uttered, "Goodbye."

Lee's Farewell to his Army

Hd.qrs. Army of N. Va.
April 10, 1865

General Orders
No. 9

After four years of arduous service marked by unsurpassed courage and fortitude, the Army of Northern Virginia has been compelled to yield to overwhelming numbers and resources.

I need not tell the brave survivors of so many hard fought battles, who have remained steadfast to the last, that I have consented to this result from no distrust of them; but feeling that valor and devotion could accomplish nothing that could compensate for the loss that must attend the continuance of the contest, I determined to avoid the useless sacrifice of those whose past services have endeared them to their countrymen.

By the terms of the agreement, officers and men can return to their homes and remain until exchanged. You will take with you the satisfaction that proceeds from the consciousness of duty faithfully performed; and I earnestly pray that a Merciful God will extend to you His blessing and protection.

With an unceasing admiration of your constancy and devotion to your Country, and a grateful remembrance of your kind and generous consideration for myself, I bid you all an affectionate farewell.

R.E. Lee
Genl.

The Assassination of Lincoln

John Wilkes Booth came from a theatrical background. His father, Junius Booth, had acted on the English stage before deserting his wife and child and coming to America with a Covent Garden flower girl in 1821. Settling in Maryland, Junius Booth resumed his acting career and began a new family--although he would not marry the mother of these children until three decades later.

In 1838, John Wilkes Booth was born. Like his brother Edwin, John followed in his father's footsteps and, by the time of the Civil War, he had achieved renown in the theater. His striking good looks won him the affection of the ladies and the envy of the gentlemen.

Booth had strong Southern sympathies, but he never served in the Confederate army, possibly because he had promised his mother he would not go to war. Instead, while the conflict raged elsewhere, the young thespian lived the comfortable life of a stage star, and, in November 1863, he even performed for the man he would later kill, Abraham Lincoln.

As Rebel fortunes failed on the field of battle, Booth began dreaming of a bold stroke that could reverse the course of the conflict. Casting himself in the lead role, he decided to kidnap Lincoln and hustle him off as a hostage to Richmond.

Through the fall of 1864, Booth assembled a catch-all crew of conspirators, including childhood friends and a part-time Confederate courier named John Surratt. Booth even traveled to Canada where he is believed to have met with Confederate agents.

By the time of Lee's surrender at Appomattox , the kidnap plot had fallen apart, and Booth's thoughts turned to assassination.

Shortly after ten p.m. on Good Friday, April 14, Booth entered the unguarded Presidential Box at Ford's Theater where Abraham and Mary Lincoln sat watching a comedy called *Our American Cousin*. Booth fired his .44 caliber derringer into the back of the president's head and slashed his knife at Major Henry Rathbone, a guest in the president's box. The athletic assassin then leapt twelve feet to the stage, but, in the process, caught his spur in one of the flags decorating the box. This threw him off-balance and the awkward landing broke his left leg.

A startled audience watched in confusion and then horror as Booth dramatically shouted, "Sic Semper Tyrannis!"--Thus ever to tyrants--and limped off the stage to escape.

Lincoln's wound was mortal. Carried to a modest private house across the street from Ford's Theater, he survived until 7:22 a.m., Saturday morning. A jubilant nation celebrating the end of war plunged headlong into grief. For the first time, a President of the United States had died at an assassin's hand.

As the drama unfolded in Ford's Theater, another assassination attempt took place at Secretary of State William Seward's mansion on Lafayette Square near the White House. A large, strange man rang the doorbell. He told the servant who answered that he had medicine which must be delivered personally to Seward, then recuperating from a serious carriage accident.

The servant objected, but the stranger pushed into the house and made his way toward Seward's bed chamber. In the melee that followed, the stranger stabbed the ailing secretary of state and injured his two sons as well as an army aide and a State Department messenger. All of the victims survived.

The assailant escaped. He was Lewis Paine, a former Confederate soldier who had joined Booth's gang.

One other assassination had been planned for that evening. George Atzerodt, a 29-year-old German immigrant, was assigned to kill Andrew Johnson in his room at the Kirkwood Hotel. Atzerodt got drunk in the hotel bar instead.

Secretary of War Edwin Stanton directed the extensive nationwide dragnet that followed. In several Northern towns, individuals who had the misfortune of sharing Booth's handsome features found themselves under suspicion. But the real assassin, despite his broken leg, managed to elude capture for twelve days as he made his way through southern Maryland and into Virginia, using the same route often followed by Confederate agents and smugglers.

On April 26, Booth's luck ended. Union cavalry trapped him in a burning tobacco barn near Port Royal, Virginia. Refusing to surrender, Booth was either shot by one of his pursuers or he shot himself. In his last moments, he asked the Federals to deliver a message: "Tell Mother I died for my country."

The rest of the conspirators were quickly rounded up. Following a military trial, four received sentences of death by hanging: Lewis Paine, who had attacked the secretary of state; George Atzerodt, who had failed to attack the vice president; David Herold, who had accompanied Booth during his escape; and Mary Surratt, the mother of Confederate courier John Surratt. Mrs. Surratt owned the boarding house where the conspirators often met and she became the first woman ever executed by the United States Government. To many, then and now, her sentence was unwarranted. In all likelihood, her actual involvement, if any, in Booth's plot was minimal.

Others of Booth's acquaintance, with varying degrees of guilt and innocence, received lengthy prison sentences. John Surratt, who had been in Elmira, New York, at the time of Lincoln's death, escaped abroad.

Abraham Lincoln was dressed for burial in the brand new suit which he had worn to his second inauguration only the month before. Funeral services took place in the East Room of the White House and then his body was moved to the capitol rotunda, making Lincoln the first person to be so honored. After that came a 1700-mile rail journey back home to Illinois, with stops in major cities along the way so that millions of grief-stricken Americans could pay their last respects.

On May 4, Lincoln was finally entombed in Springfield. As Edwin Stanton said on the morning after the assassination, "Now he belongs to the ages."

Mary Lincoln never recovered from the horror of her husband's murder. Ten years later, Robert Lincoln signed papers committing his mother to an asylum.

John Wilkes Booth fleeing after shooting Lincoln (Library of Congress)

Lincoln's casket in the rotunda of the national capitol. (U.S. Army Military History Institute)

An early 1862 pose of Joseph Eggleston Johnston before the war took its toll. (Sergeant Kirkland's Museum and Historical Society)

The War Ends:
Reunion and Reconstruction

On April 26, General Joseph Eggleston Johnston surrendered his army to William Sherman at the Bennett Farmhouse near Durham, North Carolina. One by one, the remaining Confederate forces followed suit and, on June 23, the Cherokee Indian leader, Stand Watie, became the last Rebel general to lay down arms.

Jefferson Davis fled through the South as his government fell apart around him. He hoped to escape to the trans-Mississippi area and, somehow, continue the struggle, but, on May 10, Yankee cavalry captured the Confederate president near Irwinville, Georgia. Taken in chains to Fortress Monroe, Davis endured a two-year imprisonment while the Federals considered putting him on trial for treason. Finally, his plight aroused the sympathy of a number of influential Northerners and he was released. Until his death in 1889, he struggled to find financial security and to justify the righteousness of the "Lost Cause." His two-volume book, *The Rise and Fall of the Confederate Government*, is one of the most ponderous tomes ever written about the war.

Robert E. Lee returned to Richmond where he was besieged by well-wishers wanting to see the defeated hero. That fall, he accepted the presidency of Washington College in Lexington, Virginia, believing that, in that capacity, he could best help to heal the scars of war and prepare a new generation to rebuild the South's shattered fortunes.

But the long years of battle and the heartbreak of Appomattox had taken their toll. The great grey chieftain passed away at the age of sixty-three in October, 1870.

For U.S. Grant, the post-war years held all the rewards a grateful nation could offer. Elected to the presidency in 1868, he served two terms, but Grant's political skills were far below his military abilities and his administration was marred by scandal.

Leaving office, he went on a world tour and contemplated making a third run for the White House. He lost a fortune in bad investments and, stricken with throat cancer, spent his final days writing his memoirs in the hope they would bring in enough money to provide for his family. In July, 1885, just after finishing the final lines of text, Grant died. Today his *Personal Memoirs* are widely regarded as an American military classic.

1901 and 1889 Gettysburg Union veteran's reunion ribbons. (Author's Collection. Photo by Brenda Goodhart.)

For the nation at large, it would take decades to recover from the upheaval of the fratricidal fighting. Much of the South lay in ruins. Weary Confederate soldiers who made their way home found themselves confronted not only with the task of finding a livelihood in a devastated land but also with a much different social order.

Federal troops occupied the rebellious states, and persons of color were no longer slaves. Enterprising and often unscrupulous outsiders--called "carpetbaggers" after their cloth valises--tried to manipulate the tense, unsettled atmosphere for political and financial gain.

The Federal authorities prohibited former Confederates from wearing any badge of rebellion, and many soldiers, lacking much of a wardrobe except their old uniforms, were forced to either cover or cut the brass military buttons from their coats.

SEE PG. 164

A rare photograph of a black Confederate veteran, wearing many of his reunion ribbons. (Sergeant Kirkland's Museum and Historical Society)

The secret society known as the Ku Klux Klan made its first appearance in December 1865. These white-robed nightriders, pretending to be the ghosts of Confederate dead, waged a clandestine campaign of terror against blacks and others who were seen as threatening the values of the old South. Finally, the violence grew to be too much even for their Grand Wizard, former Confederate Lieutenant General Nathan Bedford Forrest, and, by 1869, he had officially dissolved the organization.

Violence flared in New Orleans, too. In 1874, a group of recalcitrant ex-Rebels, known as the White League, took on the civil authorities, routing the police and black militia during a melee in the center of the city. Federal troops restored order.

Gradually the hatred of war gave way to the prosperity of peace and, in Congress, the power of vengeful Radical Republicans gradually faded. Former Confederates were again allowed to hold political office, and many of the old military leaders went on to serve in Southern state houses and in Washington. Wartime heroes James Longstreet and John Mosby scandalized their Confederate comrades when they cast their support for the Republican candidate, U.S. Grant, in the 1868 presidential elections.

In 1877, the last of the occupying troops left what had been the Confederacy and home rule was restored to the South. If the scars and bitterness of the conflict had not quite been erased, this at least marked some form of closure. By the time of the Spanish-American War in 1898, former grey general Joe Wheeler was serving as a general in the U.S. Army. Going once again into battle, the excited old soldier surprised his men by urging them to whip the "Yankees."

For the persons of color who had so recently been slaves, the end of servitude marked a strange new beginning. For a time, the Freedman's Bureau created schools and provided social services and civil protections for the newly emancipated. But the bureau gradually withered due to political in-fighting in Washington and the former slaves were left to make their own way in the world. Some stayed on as sharecroppers at the same plantations they had worked before the war, no longer in chains but still tied economically to their old masters. Others migrated north to seek a new life outside Dixie.

The victorious Federal armies celebrated the war's end with a massive, two-day parade down Pennsylvania Avenue in the nation's capital. Then the grizzled heroes of so many hard-fought battles, battles in which they had preserved the United States, were mustered out of service to return home. For most of the survivors, the biggest adventure of their lives was over.

However, they would not forget. Early in 1866, the Grand Army of the Republic was founded and chapters quickly opened across the country. This Northern veteran's association soon became politically potent, helping to elect presidents, governors and congressmen. Wags said that GAR really meant "Generally All Republicans," for what ex-soldier could ever vote against the party of Lincoln? In all, five former Union officers eventually occupied the White House. Not until a hundred years after the conflict would a resident of what had been the old Confederacy be elected chief executive.

Southerners, too, felt the need to maintain the bonds forged in battle, and the United Confederate Veterans Association was formed in 1889. The annual encampments of both the GAR and UCV gave the old soldiers a chance to relive their days of glory and talk about times past.

There was always the unseen presence of those who did not survive. In total, approximately 650,000 Americans died in the struggle, and total casualties went well above one million.

The practice of decorating the graves of the fallen began shortly after the war in both North and South, evolving into what we now know as Memorial Day. Every town of any size felt obligated to erect a soldiers' monument at the courthouse or at the cemetery.

Of course, some of those who survived the butchery never recovered from their wounds. Amputees abounded. In the year after the war, artificial limbs were the single largest item in the Mississippi state budget.

The Civil War forever changed the United States, though many of the issues which brought about the fighting remain with us in one form or another even today. Looking back through the growing mists of time, it is difficult to truly appreciate the enormity of the sacrifice made by the men and women on both sides of this tragic conflict. Even as the old battlefields are shamelessly bulldozed for strip malls and fast-food restaurants, it is little wonder that so many of us remain in awe of the courage and valor of these earlier Americans.

Southerners prepare for the unveiling of the Robert E. Lee monument in Richmond, Virginia, on May 29, 1890. (US Army Military History Institute)

Searching for Your Civil War Relatives

As a child, when my interest in the Civil War was just beginning, my grandmother told me that I had a relative who had fought in the conflict. Naturally, I wanted to know more, so we went off to see his grave in a small, country churchyard near McAlevy's Fort, Pennsylvania.

I was lucky. My ancestor's tombstone contained a great deal of information. His name was Lieutenant James P. Gibboney, Company C of the 45th Pennsylvania Volunteer Infantry, and he lost his life on July 18, 1864, outside Petersburg, Virginia.

With his name and regiment, additional records were easy to obtain from the state archives. A visit to a local library uncovered the multi-volume Bates' *History of the Pennsylvania Volunteers*, which contains information on every Pennsylvania regiment. Eventually, at a relic show, I found a copy of the long out-of-print *History of the 45th Pennsylvania Veteran Volunteer Infantry*. Many units, both North and South, published post-war histories, and these can be a treasure trove of information.

Learning of my interest, distant relatives sent me copies of the information they had gathered, including rare news-clips and outlines of a family tree that traced my forbears to their American arrival in the early 1700's. In recent years, I used the research service of Sergeant Kirkland's Historical Society in Fredericksburg, Virginia, to obtain photocopies of my Civil War ancestor's service records from the National Archives.

This example illustrates the basic steps anyone can take to explore his or her family's past. First off, ask relatives what they know. Then use that information to open other sources.

The keys to success are your Civil War ancestor's name, regiment and state. If you have those, you can access the service records of the National Archives for both Union and Confederate soldiers. The National Archives also has the pension records for Union troops. Some Southern states paid pensions to former Confederates, so if your relative wore grey, investigate your state archives as well.

I found it easiest to pay a small fee and have Sergeant Kirkland's obtain the National Archives records for me. On the other hand, you can write to the archives, request NATF Form 80, complete the form, and return it to the archives. They will then send an invoice for record copying fees which must be paid before they will mail the information to you.

The address for the National Archives is: General Reference Branch (NNRG-P), National Archives and Records Administration, 7th and Pennsylvania Avenue, NW, Washington, DC 20408.

What if you don't have your ancestor's name, regiment or state? What if you are just wondering if you had a relative who fought in the war? This calls for real detective work. You must begin the painstaking process of creating a family tree, working backwards until you can get to the 1860's. Then you'll have the names of relatives who may have fought in the war, which will give you a starting point for your research.

Again, the first step is to talk to your relatives, and getting as many names as far back as you can. Check old family Bibles which often contain entries of births and deaths. Courthouse marriage and property records will help to fill in the gaps. Federal census records can trace family members back decades before the Civil War.

Keep in mind that literacy was often a haphazard thing in the 1860's so the spelling of names can vary, even within the same document. My Civil War ancestor's last name was spelled five different ways in his records.

Contact your local historical society, too. Ask what reference materials they may have to help you and find out if any of their members are particularly adept at genealogical research. You may find an ally, who can show you short cuts to saving time.

The internet is becoming increasingly valuable for tracing family trees. Some services even offer genealogy chat groups. Plans are underway to create an accessible data-base which will, eventually, list the names and basic information for all Union and Confederate soldiers who fought in the war.

Finally, remember that not everyone is related to Robert E. Lee or U.S. Grant. A friend of mine recently obtained his ancestor's Civil War records. The soldier in question was drafted late in 1864, when he was well into his 30's, and sent off to join Sherman's army for the final few months of the war. His service record consists primarily of several long hospital stays. His maladies appear to have ended when the war did, after which he returned home to live a long and happy life.

Glossary

ABOLITIONIST--Person favoring the elimination of slavery. In New England, this movement was particularly strong.

ARMY ORGANIZATION--In the Civil War military, a company of roughly one hundred men formed the smallest military unit. Ten companies made up a regiment, and two or more regiments made up a brigade. Two or more brigades made a division, and two or more divisions formed a corps. Two or more corps comprised an army.

ARTILLERY--One of the three principal fighting branches of the Civil War army. The Napoleon--a smooth-bore, muzzleloading gun firing a twelve-pound ball--was the primary cannon used by this branch.

BLOCKADE--A corridor of Federal ships placed around the Southern coast to prevent the export of cotton and the import of arms and equipment.

CARPETBAGGERS--Unscrupulous Northerners who came south to profit from the region's post-war political and economic turmoil, these men were named after their cloth traveling bags.

CAISSON--The horse-drawn, two-wheeled vehicle used to haul cannons and hold ammunition.

CAVALRY--One of the three principal fighting branches of the Civil War army. Mounted on horseback, men of the cavalry were used to screen troop movements and scout the enemy's position.

CONTRABAND--A nickname for slaves freed by the movement of the Northern army. Since slaves were considered property, when captured by the blue forces, they were considered "contraband of war."

COPPERHEAD--A Northerner who favored a negotiated peace and sympathized with the Southern cause. The movement was particularly strong in the Midwest.

EARTHWORKS--Trenches and artillery emplacements used to protect soldiers and cannons from enemy fire.

FEDERAL--A supporter of the national government, a Unionist.

FLANK--The end of an army's line in battle, i.e., left flank, right flank. Turning an enemy's flank was a basic combat move.

FREEDMAN'S BUREAU--Created in 1865 to provide governmental assistance to newly freed slaves.

FOOT CAVALRY--A nickname for "Stonewall" Jackson's troops based upon their fast marching during the Shenandoah Valley Campaign of 1862.

GALVANIZED YANKEE--A Confederate prisoner who joined the Northern army and was sent west to guard against Indian raids.

GRAPE AND CANISTER--Deadly scatter-shot projectiles fired from cannons into advancing enemy troops.

GUERRILLAS--Irregular raiders, often informally organized, whose tactics were based upon surprise.

HARDTACK--The butt of many a soldiers' joke, this square cracker was a quarter-inch thick and made of unleavened flour. It substituted for bread when the army was on the march.

HOMESPUN--A rough fabric of wool or cotton, often homemade, that was used in various shades of grey and butternut for Confederate uniforms.

INFANTRY--One of the three principal fighting branches of the Civil War army; foot soldiers who carried muskets.

IRONCLAD--An iron-covered fighting ship.

KING COTTON--A pre-war term indicating the importance of Southern-grown cotton as both a domestic farm product and an export to the world market.

MILITIA--Local home guards, not generally the best troops.

MINIÉ BALL--The standard infantry bullet used by North and South, it was named after a French army captain who helped develop it.

MUSKET--Generic name for the basic single-shot infantry weapon of the Civil War.

NAPOLEONIC TACTICS--A style of fighting which favored the movement of block formations of men marching shoulder-to-shoulder into battle. Though this style of fighting was the norm during the war, it was rapidly becoming outdated due to the increased killing power of rifled muskets and cannons.

PICKET--Soldiers sent on outpost duty to guard against a surprise attack.

RAMROD--The rod used to push a bullet, ball, or shell down the barrel of a musket or cannon.

RECONSTRUCTION--An era in the post-war South, ending in 1877, during which the rebellious states were "reconstructed" as part of the Union.

ROUT—When an army fled from the enemy in great confusion and disorder.

SANITARY COMMISSION--The Civil War version of the USO, dedicated to providing comfort and aid for the Northern soldiers.

SECESSIONIST--A person in favor of dissolving the Union.

SEE THE ELEPHANT--Soldier slang for having been in battle. Probably derived from the punch-line of an obscure joke.

SIEGE--The process of surrounding an enemy-held city and starving it into surrender.

TRANS-MISSISSIPPI--The vast Confederate territory west of the Mississippi that was cut-off from the eastern Confederacy after the Union gained control of the river in 1863.

ZOUAVE--Soldiers who wore colorful, French-inspired uniforms with short jackets, baggy pants, gaiters and a fez or turban. Not the most practical costume for combat, it was most often seen in the early days of the war.

While visiting a dying Union soldier in Washington, D.C., Walt Whitman stated, "These hospitals, so different from all others — these thousands, and tens and twenties of thousands of American young men..." (National Portrait Gallery)

A Selected Bibliography

Battles and Leaders of the Civil War. Edison, NJ: Castle Books Edition. No dates given.

Boatner, III. Mark Mayo. *The Civil War Dictionary.* New York: David McKay Co., 1959.

Bishop, Jim. *The Day Lincoln Was Shot.* New York: Harper & Brothers, 1955.

Bowley, Freeman S. *A Boy Lieutenant.* Fredericksburg, VA: Sgt. Kirkland's, 1997.

Buchanan, Lamont. *A Pictorial History of the Confederacy.* New York: Bonanza Books, 1951.

Brownlee, Richard S. *Gray Ghosts of the Confederacy.* Baton Rouge: Louisiana State University Press, 1958.

Catton, Bruce. *The Coming Fury.* New York: Doubleday & Co., 1961.
_____ . *Terrible Swift Sword.* New York: Doubleday & Co., 1963.
_____. *Never Call Retreat.* New York: Doubleday & Co., 1965.

Cullen, Joseph P. *Where A Hundred Thousand Fell.* Washington: National Park Service, 1966.

Davis, William C. *Jefferson Davis: The Man and His Hour.* New York: Harper Collins, 1991.
_____. *The Cause Lost.* Lawrence, Kansas: University Press of Kansas, 1996.

Editors of Time-Life. *Echos of Glory: Illustrated Atlas of the Civil War.* Alexandria, VA: Time-Life, 1991.

Faust, Patricia L. *Historical Times Illustrated Encyclopedia of the Civil War.* New York: Harper & Row, 1986.

Fellman, Michael. *Citizen Sherman.* New York: Random House, 1995.

Forman, Stephen M. *A Guide to Civil War Washington.* Washington: Elliott & Clark, 1995.

Freeman, Douglas Southall. *Lee.* Abridgement by Richard Harwell. New York: Collier Books, 1961.
_____. *Lee's Lieutenants .* New York: Charles Scribner's Sons, 1944.

Furgurson, Ernest B. *Chancellorsville, 1863: The Souls of the Brave.* New York, Vintage Books, 1992.

Garrison, Webb. *Unusual Persons of the Civil War.* Fredericksburg, VA: Sgt. Kirkland's, 1996.

Grant, U.S. *Personal Memoirs of U.S. Grant.* New York: World Publishing Reprint, 1952.

Greene, A. Wilson and Gallagher, Gary W. *National Geographic Guide to the Civil War National Battlefield Parks.* Washington: National Geographic Society, 1992.

Groom, Winston. *Shrouds of Glory.* New York: Pocket Books, 1996.

Hanson, Joseph Mills. *Bull Run Remembers.* Prince William, VA: Prince William County Historical Commission Reprint, 1991.

Harris, Lt. Wm. C. *Prison-Life in the Tobacco Warehouse at Richmond.* Prince William, VA: Prince William County Historical Commission, 1994.

Henry, Robert Selph. *"First With the Most" Forrest.* Wilmington, NC: Broadfoot Publishing, 1987.

_____. *The Story of the Confederacy.* New York: Bobbs-Merrill, 1931.

Horner, Dave. *The Blockade-Runners.* New York: Dodd, Mead & Co., 1968.

Jones, Virgil Carrington. *Ranger Mosby.* Chapel Hill: University of North Carolina Press, 1944.

Hughes, Nathaniel Cheairs Jr. *Bentonville.* Chapel Hill: University of North Carolina Press, 1996.

Keller, Allan. *Morgan's Raid.* New York: Collier Books, 1962.

Pohanka, Brian C. *Don Troiani's Civil War.* Mechanicsburg, PA: Stackpole Books, 1995.

Robertson, Jr., James I. *The Civil War.* Washington: U.S. Civil War Centennial Commission, 1963.

Sears, Stephen W. *To the Gates of Richmond: The Peninsula Campaign.* New York: Ticknor & Fields, 1992.

Symonds, Craig L. *Joseph E. Johnston.* New York: Norton, 1994.

Taylor, John M. *Confederate Raider.* McLean, VA: Brassey's, 1994.

Tucker, Glenn. *Chickamauga: Bloody Battle in the West.* New York: Smithmark Reprint, 1994.

_____. *High Tide at Gettysburg.* New York: Bobbs-Merill, 1968

Various Authors. *The Civil War* (28 Volumes). Alexandria, VA: Time-Life Books, 1987.

Wert, Jeffry D. *Custer.* New York: Simon & Schuster, 1996.

_____. *General James Longstreet.* New York: Simon & Schuster, 1993.

Woodworth, Steven E. *Jefferson Davis and His Generals.* Lawrence, Kansas: University Press of Kansas, 1990.

Williams, T. Harry. *P.G.T. Beauregard: Napoleon in Gray.* Baton Rouge: Louisiana State University Press, 1955.

Index

Rally Round The Flag, Boys! Rally Once Again! *Library of Congress.*

A life-long student of the American Civil War, Douglas Lee Gibboney is the author of the well-received novel, *Stonewall Jackson at Gettysburg*. His writing has also appeared in a number of newspapers and magazines, including Civil War Times Illustrated. He lives near Boiling Springs, Pennsylvania, in a farmhouse, which was raided by Confederate cavalry during the war.

5|13